COSTING NOT LESS THAN EVERYTHING

Costing not less than everything

SUSTAINABILITY AND SPIRITUALITY IN CHALLENGING TIMES

THE 2011 SWARTHMORE LECTURE

First published August 2011

Quaker Books, Friends House, 173 Euston Road, London NW1 2BJ

www.quaker.org.uk

ISBN 978 1 907123 21 4

Cover image:
'Namib', oil on canvas, © Adam Boulter 1998, www.adamboulter.co.uk

Book designed and typeset by Cox Design, Witney

Printed by Information Press Ltd, Eynsham

THE SWARTHMORE LECTURE

The Swarthmore lectureship was established by the Woodbrooke Extension Committee at a meeting held 9 December 1907: the minute of the committee providing for an "annual lecture on some subject relating to the message and work of the Society of Friends". The name Swarthmore was chosen in memory of the home of Margaret Fox, which was always open to the earnest seeker after Truth, and from which loving words of sympathy and substantial material help were sent to fellow workers.

The lectureship continues to be under the care of Woodbrooke Quaker Study Centre Trustees, and is a significant part of the education work undertaken at and from Woodbrooke.

The lectureship has a twofold purpose: first, to interpret to the members of the Society of Friends their message and mission; and second, to bring before the public the spirit, aims and fundamental principles of Friends. The lecturers alone are responsible for any opinions expressed.

The lectureship provides both for the publication of a book and for the delivery of a lecture, the latter usually at the time of Britain Yearly Meeting of the Society of Friends. A lecture related to the present book was delivered at Yearly Meeting Gathering in Canterbury on the evening of Monday 1 August 2011.

The Swarthmore Lecture Committee can be contacted via the Clerk, c/o Woodbrooke Quaker Study Centre, 1046 Bristol Road, Selly Oak, Birmingham B29 6LJ.

Woodbrooke
Quaker Study Centre

The earth is the Lord's,
and the fulness thereof;
the world,
and they that dwell therein.

Psalm 24 (King James Bible)

CONTENTS

ACKNOWLEDGMENTS

I would like to thank the Swarthmore Lecture Committee for inviting me to write this book and deliver the lecture – a one-time opportunity and privilege to be able to say something to Friends and others on a topic of enormous importance. In particular I thank the two committee members who liaised with me throughout the process: Liz Gladstone and Jan Arriens. I am grateful to Blake Humphries and Sarah Stokes, from Quaker Communications, for their technical expertise and assistance; and to Deborah Padfield for her editorial skill.

Thanks also to Janet Morley, Funtz Michener, John Nicholson and Cliodhna Mulhern, who read and commented on an early draft of this book; to Joycelin Dawes, who read successive drafts with close attention and offered invaluable feedback; and to Zélie Gross, whose detailed suggestions have immeasurably improved the text. Any remaining deficiencies are my sole responsibility.

Kevin Redpath's contribution to the spoken lecture was a delight, and visible to everyone: I thank him.

I thank my colleagues at Woodbrooke for their support, and assistance when asked, during the process of writing. In particular, thanks to Lizz Roe; the joint work that she and I did, in creating what became The Good Lives Project, has influenced every chapter here. Also, Jennifer Barraclough, without whose fundraising skills the Project would have been a much smaller thing; and the George Cadbury Fund, whose generosity made it all possible.

And lastly – but actually the beginning – thanks to my long-standing F/friend Deborah Page, and her late mother, Helen Goom, who first took me to a Quaker meeting for worship in Derby, more than 40 years ago.

INTRODUCTION

The opening verse of Psalm 24,

> The earth is the Lord's, and the fulness thereof; the world,
> and they that dwell therein,

reminds us of our Quaker assertion that there is no separation between the sacred and the secular: that all times, all places, all beings, all actions, all thoughts, all intentions are in the realm of the sacred. Everything 'belongs to God'. This has been a lodestone of the spiritual life since long before George Fox – Fox reminded his generation, and also reminds us, of what has perhaps always been known.

History has presented *us* with a choice: we have a planetary emergency[1] and we therefore need the generations who are alive now to have a true sense of mission, of leading, of **concern*** in the Quaker sense. Earlier generations worked against slavery, for instance, or for democracy; this matter is our work to do. We, who are alive now, are truly powerful – it is our moment now. We have the knowledge and we have the technology, and after us it is too late. Can we find joy and gratitude for the challenge that faces us?

To write a book concerning any of the technical or political details about **climate change** or **peak oil** is to be certain that it will be out of date before it is published. New observations of climate-influenced phenomena are being made all the time, and the political context is highly volatile. The general gist of the situation is this: in relation to climate change, events are moving much more quickly than had previously been anticipated. Ideas for new technologies, to replace our dependence on oil, to reduce our **carbon emissions**, or to mitigate the effects of climate change, are being announced almost daily. Our international political processes are stalled, the only existing treaty (the **Kyoto Protocol**) being ineffective, with nothing in the pipeline to replace it when it expires in 2012; the 2010 negotiations in Cancún (Mexico) did nothing to change this.

---

* Terms shown in boldface are explained in the Glossary. They are printed in bold on the first occasion when they appear.

And the summer melting of the north polar icecap is opening up the possibility of deep-sea oil extraction above the Arctic Circle, adding to the cycle of warming produced by burning **fossil fuels**.

I am not attempting to address these matters – they are well-enough covered in the quality news media, online, and in regular book-publishing activity.

Rather I hope in this book to engage all of us in contemplation and re-evaluation of the profound psychological, social and spiritual crisis that we are facing; and, as a consequence, move us to change our own lives, to engage our Quaker communities and to act in the wider social and political sphere. We are going to be tested: as individuals, as families, as communities, as nations and as the whole tribe of humanity. We, Quakers in Britain, will be tested as a religious body. And the outcome is uncertain; just as in the early seventeenth century, when the Pilgrim families set off for the New World, we do not know what awaits us, we do not know if we will survive. As it says in the "Cheerful disclaimer" on the **Transition** Network website:[2]

> We truly don't know if this will work. Transition is a social experiment on a massive scale. What we are convinced of is this: if we wait for the governments, it'll be too little, too late; if we act as individuals, it'll be too little; but if we act as communities, it might just be enough, just in time.

In modern times there have been, arguably, three major crises that have undermined our view of ourselves as rational beings. The first was the carnage of the World War I trenches. The second was the liberation of the Nazi concentration camps in the spring of 1945, revealing to the world the reality of what had gone on. The third was the dropping of the atomic bombs on Hiroshima and Nagasaki in August 1945, facing us with the knowledge of our capacity for terrible, potentially global destruction. In each of these cases, the 'ordinary person' could look at the political or military leaders, at what 'they' were doing, or had done, and blame someone else.

In his memoir *The last fighting tommy*, Harry Patch[3] describes how his team of World War I gunners decided together that, as the

German foot soldiers were as much victims of the situation as they were themselves, they would not shoot to kill. They would aim for the legs, and the injured Germans would be stretchered off the battlefield, hopefully to survive the war. So, even though they were compelled to fight, and therefore were actually firing the guns, they clearly placed the responsibility elsewhere – with the politicians and generals – and sought to subvert it. They did not consider themselves to be the perpetrators of the carnage.

In the case of the Nazi concentration camps we could also point the finger at those 'others' – certainly not ourselves – who had committed these atrocities. However, there remained the nagging, shocking question: did ordinary people really not know what was happening?

In the anti-nuclear campaigning that followed the end of World War II, it was clearly someone else who was in a position to 'press the button' – we could campaign self-righteously against it.

The present situation, the fourth crisis, is different. There is no-one to point the finger at except ourselves. Those of us who live in the rich industrialised West are part of the problem, just by living. Just by getting up in the morning and going about our normal business, we are part of the problem. Even those of us who are working very hard at reducing our carbon emissions are still part of the problem. So we can campaign and protest and seek political change (and we surely need to do all of those things) but we also have to change our lives in ways that most people have barely glimpsed yet. We cannot rely on technology to enable us to continue with business as usual by other means.

So I will not be writing directly about the practicalities of current environmental issues. My focus is rather on how we make meaning and community; how we belong and how we create a home for ourselves – not just the physical home, but the emotional, psychological, cultural and spiritual home; and how we become the best we can be of the kind of species we are. I will indicate from time to time where there are matters that we as Friends, with our specific history of engagement and action, might make a particular contribution.

This book, inevitably, seeks to address a wide audience. Some readers will already be deeply engaged with and committed to these issues – I hope you will find in these pages some new facets, or dimensions, to expand your existing approach and responses. Some readers may have dipped their toe in these waters – I hope you will find here something to encourage and enable you to take further steps. Some readers may be aware that there is something to be addressed, without yet having begun to make the issues their own – I hope you will be able to find a way in through something written here.

And what of those who, having looked at the whole topic, have decided either that they don't believe it or that they choose to have nothing to do with it? For instance, the writer of a letter published in *New Scientist* (15 August 2009), who says:

> Whether or not anthropogenic climate change is a reality . . . is quite a separate issue from whether or not we should change our behaviour accordingly . . . why should any person make sacrifices for the benefit of others? In the absence of a religious or even utilitarian moral imperative there is no rational basis for demanding such a sacrifice. If climate change does not affect me personally, materially and directly, within the limited window of my remaining years, why should I care? For the record, I don't.

It is, of course, unlikely that such a person would even pick up this book; but if you do, I hope you might find something, even if only one thing, that touches your heart or opens your mind.

As an author it is always galling to be overtaken by events, between writing and publication. As a concerned human being, however, I would be delighted if everything I have written about had become commonplace by the time this is published.

A note about biblical translations

I have used a variety of different translations throughout this book. My personal preference would always be for the resonant language of the King James Bible, but that is because I grew up with it, and the rhythms of its prose are embedded in my mind and heart. It is not a translation which appeals to younger people, or to people who

were not raised in a Christian tradition – it can sound archaic, is
sometimes difficult to understand, and is full of stubbornly male
and authoritarian language. So I have chosen, for each quotation, a
translation that seems to fit best with the use to which I am putting
the quotation at that point. There is, in my view, no single translation that works well for everything.

ERV	English Revised Version
ESV	English Standard Version
KJV	King James Version
NIV	New International Version
NLT	New Living Translation
RSV	Revised Standard Version.

A note about web references
In the Notes and Further Resources sections there are a number
of references to webpages. These were all correct and accessible at
time of going to press.

A note about the endnotes
The numbered notes for each chapter are more than just references
for what is being said – together they form a significant bank of resources on the issues addressed in this book. The Further Resources
section towards the end does not repeat information already given
in the notes.

CHAPTER 1

Only one Earth

The Earth is a tiny and fragile world.
It needs to be cherished.

Carl Sagan, 1980

Earthrise (NASA, 1968)

This image divides the readers of this book into two groups: those old enough to remember the breathtaking, emotional and spiritual impact of this photograph when we first saw it; and those young enough to have grown up in a world in which this image, and others like it, already existed – who grew up having never known the world without these images being part of the picture.

Writing in 1980, astrophysicist Carl Sagan captioned this image:

> The home planet of an emerging technical civilization, struggling to avoid self-destruction. This world is observed from a temporary outpost near its lone natural satellite.[1]

Prior to the launch of the first moon shot, there had been discussions with media people in Washington to decide a suitable message to be beamed back to Earth when the Apollo 8 crew circled the moon on Christmas Eve 1968.

But when the time came, it was the astronauts themselves who decided what they would say. No-one on Earth could prevent them.

There was an eight-minute communications blackout while the spacecraft flew around the dark side of the moon, the hemisphere facing away from the Earth.

When the craft reappeared and communication was restored, one of the crew started reading their message back to the ground-crew on Earth, and to a truly massive live TV audience all round the world:

In the beginning God created the heaven and the earth. And the earth was without form, and void; and darkness was upon the face of the deep. And the Spirit of God moved upon the face of the waters.

And God said, Let there be light: and there was light. And God saw the light, that it was good: and God divided the light from the darkness. And God called the light Day, and the darkness he called Night. And the evening and the morning were the first day.

And God said, Let there be a firmament in the midst of the waters, and let it divide the waters from the waters. And God made the firmament, and divided the waters which were under the firmament from the waters which were above the firmament: and it was so. And God called the firmament Heaven. And the evening and the morning were the second day.

And God said, Let the waters under the heaven be gathered together unto one place, and let the dry land appear: and it was so. And God called the dry land Earth; and the gathering together of the waters called he Seas: and God saw that it was good.

The astronauts read from the King James Bible, and then ended with:

> And from the crew of Apollo 8, we close with good night, good luck, merry Christmas, and God bless all of you – all of you on the good Earth.

Their impulse to read this passage resonates with the much earlier views of Carl Jung. In 1944, ill in hospital and suffering a heart attack, Jung had a near-death experience in which he seemed to himself to be out in space looking back at the Earth – remember that at this time no actual images of this view existed. His vision, later described in *Memories, dreams, reflections*, was startlingly accurate:

> Far below I saw the globe of the Earth, bathed in a gloriously blue light. I saw the deep blue sea and the continents. Far below my feet lay Ceylon, and in the distance ahead of me the subcontinent of India. My field of vision did not include the whole Earth, but its global shape was plainly distinguishable and its outlines shone with a silvery gleam through that wonderful blue light. In many places the globe seemed colored, or spotted dark green like oxidized silver. Far away to the left lay a broad expanse – the reddish-yellow desert of Arabia; it was as though the silver of the Earth had there assumed a reddish-gold hue. Then came the Red Sea, and far, far back – as if in the upper left of a map – I could just make out a bit of the Mediterranean. My gaze was directed chiefly toward that.[2]

For Jung, this view, prefiguring the view of the whole globe, which he could not quite see in his vision, was the first glimpse of the Earth as a mandala figure: a circle symbolising wholeness, somewhat in the same way that the Hebrew word *shalom* signals not just 'peace' as in the most frequent translation, but also health, wholeness, completeness, perfection.

Although 'Earthrise' was the first of the famous photographs of Earth from space, arguably the most influential image to come out of the whole American space programme was the 1972 image sent back by Apollo 17.

(© NASA, 1972)

This image was known as 'The Blue Marble' and came to be the most widely reproduced image in all history. It was used by environmental campaigning groups, by commercial organisations, in advertisements, on book covers, on stickers, postcards and more. The view of the world alone in the blackness of space touched something, touched a nerve. In one campaigning advertisement the photo was reproduced with the Earth the exact size of an old pre-decimal British penny, with the slogan "Here is the Earth – don't spend it all at once". The photograph was widely sold as a postcard with a one-word caption, "Home", and on another one with the words "Love Your Mother".

If that single image were to grip the popular imagination for the first time today, we would be able to find the many versions of it all over the World Wide Web. But this was long before the Web was even imagined – we have only people's recollections and a few artefacts that happen to have survived.

But although 'The Blue Marble' was the most used, the 'Earthrise' image was the first photograph seen, and that is the one credited by Al Gore with starting the modern environment movement. It is estimated that two billion people (over half of the population of the world at that time) watched the live TV transmissions and heard the Apollo 8 crew reading the Genesis passage. And the sequence of events that followed bear out Al Gore's suggestion. After the 1968 Christmas Eve transmission:

- Friends of the Earth was founded in 1969
- the first 'Earth Day' in the USA was in 1970
- Greenpeace was founded in 1971
- the first UN summit on the environment was held in 1972 in Stockholm and the report *Limits to growth* was published, arguing that there were environmental limits to the global economy[3]
- also in 1972 the Lindisfarne Association (named after the Northumbrian monastic island) was founded in New York to "effect an evolutionary transformation of human culture"; there was a race against time – would this transformation happen before human damage to the environment became irreversible?[4]

- in 1974 Stewart Brand, originator in 1968 of *The Whole Earth Catalog*, thought better of his decision to stop publishing and brought out further editions. He also started *CoEvolution Quarterly*, which acted as a bridge between the sciences and the emerging counter-culture.

And so on – this list could extend for several pages more. Also during this period, the ideas were simmering which would be published by James Lovelock in 1979 as *Gaia: A new look at life on earth*.[5] Then in Vancouver in 1983, the churches caught up with this new consciousness when the World Council of Churches called for a "conciliar process of mutual commitment (covenant) to justice, peace and the integrity of creation" (the 'Decade for JPIC'), which became the overarching protestant ecumenical context for the pursuit of **eco-justice** for the following decade. Unlike many other WCC 'Decades', this one has not faded from sight. The churches continue to wrestle with its implications[6] – as shown most recently, perhaps, in the international interfaith conference, *Many Heavens, One Earth*, held at Windsor in November 2009, in the days before the **Copenhagen climate summit**. It was also in 1983 that Matthew Fox published *Original blessing*,[7] building on his previous decade of writing and of putting creation at the heart of spirituality.

The wonderful irony of all this is that we went to the moon, but what we discovered was the Earth. Remember that nearly all printed atlases at that time were diagrammatic, using plain colours to show national boundaries; atlases using new colour printing technology to show natural features and topography, as they might appear from space, started to appear only after the end of this first phase of the space age.

I say 'we' because of two experiences recounted by those early astronauts. The first experience, obvious to us all now, but startling in the Cold War political climate of the times, was expressed by Russian cosmonaut Oleg Makarov:

> Suddenly you get a feeling that you've never had before, that you're an inhabitant of the earth.

And Tom Stafford, of the Apollo 10 crew, said:

> You don't look down at the world as an American but as a human being.

On a later mission, Sultan Bin Salman al-Saud, the first Islamic astronaut, circling the Earth on the space shuttle, commented:

> The first day or so we all pointed to our countries. The third or fourth day we were pointing to our continents. By the fifth day we were aware of only one earth.[8]

The second experience resulted from one of the outcomes of the Apollo programme: the first astronauts to walk on the moon became major celebrities, and later went on a world tour. They recount that everywhere they went, in all parts of the world, they were greeted by people rejoicing: not that those particular men had done this thing; not that the Americans had done it; but that we – humanity – had accomplished this extraordinary feat.[9] It was truly extraordinary: those astronauts went to the moon and came back safely, with substantially less computing power on board than a mobile phone has today.[10] The decade-long Apollo programme was the largest and most expensive undertaking in the whole of human history that wasn't about waging war.

In 2008 there was a fortieth anniversary flurry of media reminiscing about the Apollo programme and about the photographs that had so impressed and affected us. It now seems hard to recall the awe they generated at the time. Surrounded as we are by a world much more populated with images than was the case in 1968, we have perhaps become jaded by so much visual stimulation and, of course, a significant fraction of us now alive has no recollection of a world without those images available.

But looking back now, the lessons and emotions of that time flow into our current concerns about climate change and other environmental threats that have magnified since then. Recalling what was stirred in many people, including those self-professed as non-religious, we need to take with utter seriousness the place of theology, religion and spirituality as necessary to our human response to the challenges facing us. People of faith, of all faiths, have a crucial role to play.

Oleg Makarov's sense of being an "inhabitant of the earth" can now be reinforced by developments in another area of science – genetics – that have occurred in the time since those space missions. The powerful combination of genetics and archaeology suggests that, after tens of thousands of years of early hominids living in Africa, all of the non-African people of this world are descended from just one group of a few hundred African ancestors who left that continent more than 100,000 years ago. There were probably many other groups who also left, but it appears that they all eventually died out. The people of modern Africa are descended from those who stayed. You may recall the widespread media attention given in 1987 to the discovery by geneticists of 'mitochondrial Eve', of the perhaps startling suggestion that the genetic heritage of humanity shows only one female lineage surviving from our earliest ancestors. There is only one Earth and only one family – we are all cousins.[11] We might look to cultures other than our own, where family relationships are reckoned differently, and where relations whom we call 'cousins' would be viewed as brothers and sisters. We are all truly one family, we are all truly brothers and sisters, not only ideologically or spiritually, but also biologically; in our flesh and bones, we are family.[12]

As Friends, we would perhaps look first to our spirituality as a response to the majestic scale of what confronts us, but we should not underestimate the place of theology in creating frameworks of meaning and purpose that can inspire and move us to action. A significant consequence of a theistic religion is the sense of human dependence – we did not make this Earth, we do not sustain it, we do not own it. Perhaps one of the most powerful statements of this comes in the Book of Job, chapter 38 – God speaks to Job (NLT):

> Where were you when I laid the foundations of the earth? . . .
> Have you ever commanded the morning to appear and caused
> the dawn to rise in the east? . . . Who created a channel for
> the torrents of rain? Who laid out the path for the lightning?
> Who makes the rain fall on barren land, in a desert where no

one lives? Who sends rain to satisfy the parched ground and make the tender grass spring up? . . .

Do you know the laws of the universe? Can you use them to regulate the earth? . . . Can you shout to the clouds and make it rain?

And on and on for several pages, God thunders at Job, who eventually replies:

You asked, "Who is this that questions my wisdom with such ignorance?" It is I – and I was talking about things I knew nothing about, things far too wonderful for me . . . I had only heard about you before, but now I have seen you with my own eyes.

This is the crucial moment, when Job *sees*: sees with his own eyes the world as God sees it; sees himself as a miniscule part of the whole creation, insignificant and ridiculous in his little human pride. I believe that it is something of this experience that the Apollo astronauts spoke of, and the millions of us around the world who watched those images beamed back were also given a tiny part of it.

What we somehow have to rediscover, we as the whole human community, is that the Earth is not ours to dispose of as we wish. Even if people cannot subscribe to a belief that "the earth is the Lord's", there are other ways of seeing that we are not the owners. We are merely tenants passing through, with the responsibility of a full repairing lease on the premises, and borrowing everything we use.

You may have heard our Friend Jocelyn Bell Burnell speak of our bodies, and of the Earth itself, being made up of the remnants of ancient exploding stars – fragments of cosmic stardust happening to coalesce just now in this configuration that we call our bodies, our homes, our gardens, our possessions.[13] A journalist recently wrote of his pregnant wife "building a child out of stardust . . . quietly waiting in hope . . . for seven pounds of stardust, borrowed from the dark."[14]

There is a saying that we do not inherit the Earth from our ancestors but rather borrow it from our children, and their children. We are currently borrowing more than can be paid back. **Earth Overshoot Day** is the point in the year when we have used up as much of the Earth's total resources as the Earth itself can regenerate in a year. Since the late 1980s we have been going into eco-deficit each year, progressively degrading the environment. In 2010 the moment of overshoot was estimated to be on 21 August (the date for 2011 was not available at the time this book went to press).[15]

Margaret Atwood has written a modern parable, a version of the story of Scrooge, in which he is visited by the ghosts of Earth Day, past, present and future. On waking after the trauma of the visitations, Scrooge reflects that:

> I don't really own anything. Not even my body. Everything I have is only borrowed . . . How do I even begin to pay back what I owe? Where should I start?[16]

CHAPTER 2

What kind of community?

Home is the place where, when you have to go there,
They have to take you in.

Robert Frost, 'The death of the hired man', 1914

The images of the Earth, discussed in Chapter 1, came only six years after the first publication of Rachel Carson's influential book *Silent spring*.[1] Even though she was labelled as hysterical and extremist by prominent figures from the chemical industry and certain members of the media, attempts to discredit Carson, by challenging her credibility as a scientist, backfired. Her work showed how pesticide use in one place spread chemical poisoning to far distant locations – DDT was found in birds all over the world, causing their eggshells to be thin and their reproductive rate to fall, hence the title of the book. She also documented the prevalence of DDT in the breast milk of women, even among groups living above the Arctic Circle, and the fact that it was transmitted to their babies. This significant book shocked many into realising for the first time that we are truly one community of all beings on the earth. The photographs from the Apollo missions added another dimension to this emerging sense of there being only one human community: you cannot see national boundaries from space.

The sense of one vast human community (6.7 billion now compared with about 4 billion then) may act as a focal point, or motivator, for some; but for most of us, our actual sense of community is much closer to home. As the effects of climate change and peak oil start to impact significantly on our own local lives, we will need to rely much more on our immediate community – the people and places within walking and cycling distance (and sometimes a bus journey) from where we live. And indeed, starting to do that before we are forced to is one of the ways of reducing carbon emissions caused by the transportation of both goods and people.

In this chapter I will consider some of the questions, issues and lessons we can draw from a wide variety of forms of **intentional community**, looking at how they inform and relate to aspects of our more usual and local contexts for community life.

You may know the film *Witness*, released in 1985 and set contemporaneously among the Amish of Pennsylvania. The film contains a violent police/criminal plot and a love interest, and stars Harrison Ford; but the real stars are the Amish. A little over half way through there is a scene in which the whole community turns out to raise a barn for a newly married couple. Apart from a little dialogue at the start and end of the scene, there is no speech. To a background soundtrack of baroque-style music, the whole community just gets on in smooth cooperation, the men raising the barn, the women preparing and serving food, the children taking cool drinks to the labouring men. Everyone knows their place and their role. Even the stranger who sojourns among them, whose presence has been a source of conflict and difficulty, seems to fit in effortlessly. The barn is raised and roofed, the community's solidarity is strengthened and affirmed.

Every time I watch it, and I have seen it numerous times, I am moved to tears by this scene; and I wonder each time what those tears are really about. When I have spoken about this with Friends I have been struck by how frequently the person I am talking to has jumped immediately to offering me an 'answer' to my question, telling me that it is quite straightforward and that what my tears are 'really' about is . . . Then follows something of that Friend's own concerns, rather than mine. Two things interest me about this repeated form of response. The first is the extraordinary assumption, by someone who does not really know me or anything about me, that she can accurately interpret some facet of my subjective experience. The second and wider issue is the repeated rush to an answer rather than a willingness to sit with the question; a lack of interest in what a question might reveal to us if we set aside the desire for an answer. The poet Rainer Maria Rilke put it like this:

> to be patient toward all that is unsolved in your heart and to try to love the *questions themselves* . . . Do not now seek the answers, which cannot be given you, because you would not be able to live them. And the point is, to live everything. Live the questions now. Perhaps you will then gradually, without noticing it, live along some distant day into the answer.[2]

The emotions stirred in me by this scene seem to be a deep yearning for something, or a kind of grief – not for something once had and then lost, but that other kind of grief, for something one has never had and never will have. It seems to be a longing for that depth of true community. I also wonder if this is a false yearning, in the way that Marx spoke of "false consciousness". If I step back from the emotion that is stirred and examine the situation rationally, would I really want to live in such a conservative community, with strict hierarchy and authority and rigid separation of gender roles? I am the product of twentieth-century Western individualism, 1960s radicalism and 1970s feminism; I also value highly my privacy and solitude. So of course the truthful answer is no, I would not actually want to live in such a way.

But the tears, the sense of yearning, nevertheless point to something important and real. This seven-minute scene, in a commercial movie, manages to evoke a deep sense of recognition that a good life – 'good' in material, ethical and spiritual ways – is very far removed from the average western lifestyle and, fundamentally, that such a life has some kind of community at its core. It is the kind of community that is like 'home' in the sense that Robert Frost uses the word in the quotation on the title page of this chapter: a place of unconditional belonging; a place that we do not have to 'earn' or 'deserve'; a place that will take us in without question;[3] a place where we know we can belong.

Such a community, such a belonging, has to be based on reserves of trust, mutuality and unselfishness – trust that one is not alone; trust that there are others who will help to make life possible. In our individualised, materialistic Western lives, those are qualities fast fading from the norms of everyday life; but more than this – and especially interesting, because it is embedded in a commercial film – the essence of the community portrayed is that it is united in serving God. The spiritual lack in Western materialistic society leaves us, collectively, without a clarity of focus and purpose, and the yearning for 'community' is one of the results.

It is beyond the scope of this chapter to give a history of the concept of intentional community, but its antecedents certainly include the ancient monastic communities (Buddhist, Christian and Sufi); other kinds of religious communities; a long line of artistic communities; a range of different types of therapeutic communities; political communes; the Kibbutz movement . . . and many more. There are many models of present-day community, each fashioned to meet the different situations – social, economic, geographic – and different needs of the individuals involved.

One thing we know from all of these examples is that creating and living in community is not easy. We have only to note that in *The Rule of St Benedict*, Chapter 70 is entitled 'That no one presume to strike another unlawfully', and includes the sentences:

> We ordain that it is not allowed to any to excommunicate or to strike any one of his brethren, except to him to whom authority shall have been given by the abbot. And let those who offend be reproved before all, that the rest be put in fear of offending.[4]

It is always instructive to note what actions and behaviours are forbidden by any institution, whether religious or secular: the fact that someone has taken the trouble to forbid them is a sure sign that they happen, perhaps frequently.

Another example, demonstrating that community is not easy, comes from much closer to home for me. There will be readers of this book who recall **Woodbrooke Quaker Study Centre** in its earlier days, before the present model of running a year-round programme of short courses and conferences. Until the end of 1999, Woodbrooke ran on a term-time basis with students resident for 11 weeks at a time, during which they formed a temporary residential community. Even over a period of less than three months, such constant close proximity was challenging. For mature students, who had their own homes and were used to an independent life, it was not at all simple to transfer to living in one room on a corridor, eating food that you had not chosen at a time you had not chosen, and being continually under the scrutiny of others. It brought back memories, perhaps of family and childhood or of boarding school or college, none of which provided models of how to live in community as an adult. I recall one student, a married woman in her mid-30s, taking a sabbatical from a demanding senior job in one of the caring professions, saying to me:

> My image of community is noise, bells, the institutional clock. I'm intrinsically a looker-after of others, not self. I'm trying to find a balance between being a helpful member of

the community and looking after myself. I don't immediately see community as nurturing me, so much as an awful lot of people that need nurturing.

The give-and-take essential to community life may be challenging in either direction, or both.

Of course community is not limited to intentional residential settings. In the religious context there is a long history of the local church congregation being community for its members in many ways, including at its best providing spiritual nurture, practical help, human fellowship and common purpose. For much of Quaker history this has been a significant dimension to the life and organisation of the Society of Friends. Indeed, the current version of our book of discipline, *Quaker faith & practice*,[5] entitles Chapter 10 'Belonging to a Quaker meeting', its first sub-heading being 'Our community', a section containing 20 extracts. The fact that the next sub-heading is 'Conflict within the meeting' tells us something else important about community, as does the fact that this section has only four entries: it is not a matter that we find easy to deal with. This is not so much about a need for 'conflict resolution' as about finding together the deep grounding of our commonality, which is deeper than mere 'agreement'. As Parker Palmer, writing in 1977, reminds us:

> In a true community we will not choose our companions, for our choices are so often limited by self-serving motives. Instead, our companions will be given to us by grace. Often they will be persons who will upset our settled view of self and world. In fact, we might define true community as the place where the person you least want to live with always lives!
>
> (Quaker faith & practice 10.19)[6]

In many of our local Quaker meetings today, there is concern about the meeting as community, and how that sense may be fostered. We are no longer a separated group, a holy community with a hedge between us and the world; we no longer live a large part of our daily lives alongside the Friends we worship with on a Sunday; we no longer have elders who come around to our houses to check our plainness of living.[7] But newcomers among us often speak of finding Friends as a kind of coming home, and it is vital that we foster our capacity to welcome and include those who seek us out, as well as making ourselves more accessible to those who might have assumed that our way is not for them.

Addressing this in practical terms, the authors of the Spiritual Hospitality Project[8] write:

> A welcoming atmosphere is not a matter of policy and pamphlets; it is in the hands of individual Friends responding to individual newcomers . . . We call upon every Friend to recognise their responsibility . . . to be sensitive and welcoming to newcomers and not-so-newcomers.

We also need to remember that community is about reciprocity, as is hospitality. Harvey Gillman reminds us[9] that *hospes* in Latin means both host and guest, and in both the monastic and the nomadic desert traditions the relationship between host and guest involves a sacred bond of mutual trust and respect. We are a community of sojourners, merely passing through; we are the current stewards, not the 'owners', of our meeting houses and other local Quaker resources, and of the ethos and reputation of Quakers. We are similarly the current stewards of the Earth, and we urgently need to start being good stewards.

One of the dilemmas about being welcoming to newcomers, and being community for and with each other in our local meetings, is finding the right balance between separateness and togetherness. Quakers as a group have a higher proportion of introverts than is the case in the surrounding society[10] – our style of worship and being together is attractive to people with introverted temperaments. So a particular challenge for Friends and perhaps, therefore, a gift we may be able to offer to others, is how to create community that works for introverts.

Alongside the concerns and efforts of Friends to nurture the community life of their local Quaker meeting, there are numbers of Quakers today engaged in forming and sustaining other kinds of intentional community. While such ventures are never likely to be the path for most of us, there are nevertheless lessons from their experience which have a broader reach, and something to say to all of us.

Roger and Susan Sawtell, Swarthmore Lecturers in 2006, wrote about their model of community at The Neighbours in Northampton. In an earlier piece,[11] Roger had described how it started and developed. He tells a story of a group growing out of their local church, meeting together in each other's houses fortnightly over ten years, for a simple meal, discussion and communion service, as well as attempting to share more – both material possessions and their hopes and fears. This grew into a desire for a shared roof, and the model of adjacent terraced houses seemed more practical than one large house. In an extraordinary sequence of events – resulting from both faith and boldness – they were able to buy three adjacent properties, which they altered to provide interconnecting doors and some shared areas, with each household still having its own front door. The community later grew to five adjacent houses, the terraced house model giving flexibility for the community to grow organically, while retaining the legally simpler pattern of separate ownership. After 23 years it was decided that the community should be laid down.

From the start, the community was ecumenical, creating a pattern of shared worship as well as some shared meals, social time, decision-making and Bible study. As the group's life together developed, the sense of community widened to embrace service to others. They offered some support to people recovering from mental illness and two young people with such problems lived in the community for several years. Roger writes:

> Our story over 20 years is not one of blinding flashes of inspiration nor sudden changes of lifestyle. Perhaps our most significant discovery is of a community consisting of adjacent terrace houses, separately owned but with flexible shared facilities and shared access. This pattern could be repeated in many roads in most towns and from such bases there would arise opportunities for material and spiritual sharing and for caring for others in many different ways.[12]

I have described The Neighbours at length because their story embodies many of the principles and practical issues that any form of intentional community (whether residential, or a group like a local meeting) must take into account – how to live together, how to deal with both legalities and practicalities, how to manage the internal life of the group, and how the group reaches out and relates to its surrounding neighbourhood. Some of the same dilemmas and approaches to solutions may be found in later ventures. In 1989, in the early days of the Quaker community in Bamford, Rachel Rowlands wrote:

> This idea of people having sufficient separate space – the families with their self-contained units, single people in individual bedsits and a flat – stems from early discussions when we recognised that many communities founder through lack of breathing space and privacy. There is still much scope for 'being communal': twice-daily meeting for worship, four o'clock tea in the main kitchen, looking after other people's children, borrowing this, lending a hand with that, communal housework, a shared meal followed by house meeting each Friday evening, entering into each other's joys and sorrows, celebrating birthdays, gardening, developing new skills together in work on the roof or down the manhole . . . We are called to recognise each other's boundaries, strengths and weaknesses, to be assertive and learn to handle conflict constructively . . . As meeting for worship is the cornerstone of our spiritual life, so these meetings are for the nitty-gritty of living together.
>
> (Quaker faith & practice 22.27)

Twenty years later, Linda Batten reflects on her own motivations, hopes and desires in joining the community at Bamford, where she lived for nine years:

My choice to live in intentional community had two main things at its heart: my desire to live alongside more like-minded people, not just in a casual house share; and my belief that communal living is more environmentally sustainable, particularly in terms of shared resources. I was looking for a spiritual community – people who understood my commitment to Quakerism, and my belief in god. Depending on who has been living here, our communal spiritual practices have changed over the years.

We have a large building, plus an old stable block and caretaker's house. From this we have created three family houses, two self-contained flats, three bed-sitting rooms and a number of single rooms with shared use of the main kitchen. There is a shared sitting room in the main house, and a separate Meeting room used primarily for worship and House Meetings. Those living in the bed-sitting and single rooms share several bathrooms. We have 11 acres of land on which we grow fruit and veg, harvest wood for log burners and maintain a wildlife area.

When I moved in I was single, so it was good to be with a mixed age group, with families and singletons. It was great to live with people who took some things for granted: composting, recycling, log burners, public transport, vegetarianism. People understood my Quaker commitments and I loved not having to explain all that.

There was a good balance of private and personal space and that was attractive to me. We shared some meals; and fortnightly, over a weekend, we worked together on the land and buildings. It wasn't always easy to live there: we had our differences; it can be frustrating waiting for the slow process of community decision making; people leave, new people join and the wheel gets reinvented. Unexpectedly, the daily 'being there' didn't feel particularly Quakerly. Perhaps because I have spent a lot of time with active Quakers, living in a Quaker Community just felt like living.

(Linda Batten has since moved out of the Quaker Community into a secular housing co-operative.)

One model of community that is currently growing in popularity and activity is cohousing. The UK Cohousing Network[13] describes this as:

> a way of living which brings individuals and families together in groups to share common aims and activities while also enjoying their own self-contained accommodation and personal

space. Cohousing communities are a means of compensating for the alienating effects of modern life where neighbours don't recognise each other and where day-to-day collaboration is minimal.

Again, this spells out some of the issues raised by Roger Sawtell, and fleshes out his suggestion that a model similar to The Neighbours could be replicated in streets and towns all over the country. Cliodhna Mulhern, a Friend just starting out on this path, describes her reasons:

For so many years we had lamented our ordered and isolated, nuclear existence so far from the chaotic and loving neighbourliness of my childhood in rural Ireland. As time passed we came so see that our lifestyle, freely chosen, was reinforcing our sense of separateness and was in some strange way holding us back from serving those around us . . . Not only that; it was also costing the Earth. If we were to live up to our own values we had to change.

Surfing the web for 'eco-housing' we found Lancaster Cohousing, an intergenerational, intentional community of 30 households building ecohomes and creating community together in a village outside Lancaster. The eight-acre site will include 30 homes, a co-house where we will share social time and meals when we choose, common gardens and allotments, a laundry, a children's room, workshops, a car pool and a large mill building converted for managed workspace for sustainable businesses. Within three months of discovering Lancaster Cohousing we had made our application, been accepted, sold our home in Chester, invested much of our freed-up capital into the project, and had moved to a small rented house in Lancaster to be part of it all.

Being part of it all means making together all the decisions that any property developer would make. For most of us this has been a steep learning curve; though with engineers, IT specialists, accountants, project management specialists, ecologists, scientists, group facilitators and health professionals in our midst this has been helped along greatly. Building our community is our other main focus – involving getting to know one another, helping one another, sharing equipment and tasks, clarifying our values, evolving our polices, learning together, working together on practical projects on our beautiful site, and keeping our spirits up. The main challenge is to keep these two – the practical building work and the community building work – in balance.

What interests me about the particular examples above is that they all involve an enhancement, a deepening and broadening, of what we might ideally hope our own neighbourhoods to be. For the vast majority of us, our community will be forged from the locality where we find ourselves living. We may have ended up in that place for a variety of reasons, some of them more consciously chosen than others, some of them standing up to more scrutiny than others. For most of us, moving to a different place to find or create community is unlikely to be our path of choice. We have to create community in the place we happen to find ourselves.

And indeed, community does have to be *created*; it does not just happen by virtue of living in close proximity with one another. The findings from a YouGov poll in mid 2010 showed that nearly half of UK adults agreed that "people know more about the daily activities of their favourite celebrity than their neighbour".[14] Much of Transition Town activity, while being stimulated by the challenges of peak oil, climate change and **energy descent**, is actually directed to the re-creation of local community, in terms of both practical activities together and enhanced relationships. And, of course, it is often the case that undertaking a real task together is a deeply effective way of building community relationships. On the Transition Culture website, this is summarised as "How might our response to peak oil and climate change look more like a party than a protest march?"[15]

One of the facets of community that Roger Sawtell's account points to is the growth of the life of the community outwards into connection with, and service to, the surrounding society. Theorists of group behaviour list "relationships with other groups" as one of the vital components for a healthy ongoing group life, so that a group does not become isolated, inward-looking, and self-absorbed. Thus, as Transition work develops, the local communities forging strong internal bonds need to remain open to other groups and influences, and not create a 'fortress' mentality that seeks to preserve their own group by excluding others:

. . . peak oil is our personal and collective call to power. This is the time when we truly find out what we can do when we collectively apply our genius and brilliance. I don't believe that our collective response to crisis will be violence and disintegration, I believe our collective adaptability, creativity and ingenuity will come to the fore.[16]

A working example of this open approach is Incredible Edible Todmorden.[17] It has taken the familiar route of many Transition and similar initiatives in focusing on local food production. Volunteer community groups are growing food in every available public space, from large and small pieces of land to municipal street planters. The food produced is free for anyone to take, enabling the community to engage in a form of urban foraging. But, as one of the founders says, "this isn't really about self-sufficiency at all; it's about community."[18]

These examples draw attention to the importance of devoting focus and energy to our local communities, but we also need to start thinking about what kind of national community we want to be, here in Britain. The current best estimates of how a warming climate will affect these islands suggest that – as a small land mass, in temperate latitudes, surrounded by ocean (a maritime climate) – we, like similar places such as Japan and New Zealand, will fare relatively well compared to many other parts of the world. We will be neither drowned nor drought-stricken.[19] This will make us, along with countries in more northern latitudes, one of the attractive destinations for the slow but inexorable stream of climate refugees from all over the globe; we will be one of the lifeboats.[20] But we are already a crowded island. If we had to be self-sufficient we would not have enough land to feed our present population, let alone a vastly increased one. Friends have a history of concern for refugees and asylum seekers. Now is the time to start preparing a response to the popular and political voices which will certainly be raised in antagonism to the needs of those beyond our shores.

This will be a very difficult dilemma: do we turn people away in order to preserve the life and health of those already here? Or do we take people in and, if so, how do we feed a growing population on a small land mass? If we take in some people but not all, how do we make those decisions? These problems are not yet pressing upon us so this relatively peaceful and non-urgent time is the moment to begin thinking long-term about this aspect of our future. As Friends we are called to have confidence in our history on these matters, and confidence in our ability to influence and to "speak truth to power".

There are other facets of community currently being explored, which already seem ubiquitous but are in reality still very new, in terms of human lifespans and generations. Virtual communities have been forming on the World Wide Web, via email lists and bulletin boards, for a few years now; blogs and other social media such as Facebook and Twitter are even more recent. We can already see some of their potential, for example in organising campaigns or protests, in keeping people informed and enabling the exchange of ideas. Links are built and communities formed between people who would never have met each other face to face, and existing friendship networks gain an additional channel. These developments are largely, though not exclusively, communities of younger people, and it is the generation now growing up with these media as a taken-for-granted part of their world ('digital natives') who will expand them beyond our current imagining.

But one word of caution: in our day-to-day experience of them, these links may seem very robust to us, but they are in fact quite fragile. The whole network on which we have come to depend with phenomenal speed (Google has been around only since 1998, Facebook since 2004 and Twitter since 2006), is completely reliant on a secure and continuous electricity supply. As we saw in early 2011 in Egypt, a political regime under pressure from a popular uprising can simply cut all communications links. Unintended power outages could rupture some or all of these connections very easily. Local power cuts – as a result of adverse weather, criminal activity or fuel shortage, for instance – will cut people off in local or regional groupings. A substantial solar storm could put out some, most or all of the planet's communications and electricity grids.[21] With a peak of solar activity expected during 2013, this is a significant threat. For all the alluring potential of virtual communities, we must be sure to maintain strong local, real-life, face-to-face communities in the places where we live and work.[22]

As Friends, we may find that the fruits of our explorations into creating and sustaining community in our meetings could become a resource for others in our local areas, as we discover together how to move towards a lower-carbon way of living. Some of our Quaker processes and practices are so familiar to us, so taken for granted, that we can forget how precious, powerful and significant they are; there are trainers and consultants who earn their living by teaching groups of people how to sit in a circle, take turns, and really listen to each other with deep, respectful listening.[23] If we are true to our Quaker principles and practices, true to our leadings and to what at best we are capable of, then we have a gift that we can offer to the wider world in this era of growing need.

Our deepest fear is not that we are inadequate; our deepest fear is that we are powerful beyond measure. It is our light, not our darkness, that most frightens us. We ask ourselves, who am I to be brilliant, gorgeous, talented, and fabulous? Actually, who are you not to be? You are a child of God. Your playing small doesn't serve the world. There is nothing enlightened about shrinking so that other people won't feel insecure around you. We were born to make manifest the glory of God that is within us. It's not just in some of us; it's in everyone. And as we let our own light shine, we unconsciously give other people permission to do the same. As we are liberated from our own fear, our presence automatically liberates others.

Marianne Williamson, quoted by Nobel Prize-winner
Nelson Mandela in his inaugural address[24]

CHAPTER 3

What does a good life look like?

Jesus said . . . Go, and do thou likewise.
Luke 10:37 (ERV)

What does a 'good life' look like? As discussed in Chapter 2, the aspirations of any form of intentional community or enhanced local neighbourhood tell us something about our dreams for the kind of life we would like to be living.

The histories of Western intellectual and religious life are not short of prescriptions for what the good life might consist of, and a number of them still resonate today with our ecological concerns. Some 3,500 years ago Moses gave the Israelites what we now call the Ten Commandments; in our twenty-first century times of environmental awareness, not coveting our neighbour's goods takes on a modern twist, as a commandment against consumerism. Seven and a half centuries after Moses, the prophet Micah gave us two well-known and well-loved models of the good life, the first a description, the second a command:

> They will beat their swords into plowshares and their spears into pruning hooks. Nation will not take up sword against nation, nor will they train for war anymore. Everyone will sit under their own vine and under their own fig tree, and no one will make them afraid.
>
> *(Micah 4:3–4)*

> He has shown you, O mortal, what is good. And what does the LORD require of you? To act justly and to love mercy and to walk humbly with your God.
>
> *(Micah 6:8)*[1]

Micah's version of what God requires of us has led to a world-wide movement of churches and Christian agencies uniting to hold their governments to account for the promises they made towards the fulfilment of the Millennium Development Goals[2] of eradicating extreme poverty and hunger by 2015. This movement, The Micah Challenge, has a UK section which states its aims as:

> [seeking] transformational change in society, through the active involvement of the church with the poor and against the injustices of poverty. It seeks to sensitise and engage

Christians into greater political and practical involvement with the issues relating to poverty by highlighting biblical truths which prompt a compassion of heart. It will also enable Christians to pray, take action, speak out and engage with the issues surrounding poverty, here in the UK as well as overseas.[3]

A century and a half after Micah, the Buddha enunciated the idea of Right Livelihood: that we should not make our living by activities that harm others, and thus should actively seek a profession that causes no harm. This is part of the Buddha's fourth Noble Truth which, in its entirety, might be seen as a broader guide to the good life: Right Understanding or Views; Right Thought; Right Speech; Right Action; Right Livelihood; Right Effort; Right Mindfulness; and Right Concentration. The third, fourth and fifth of these represent ethical conduct; the sixth, seventh and eighth, mental discipline. The first two represent 'wisdom', the philosophical underpinning of the whole: the insight that we are all radically interconnected, that no thing or being exists as a separate entity and, therefore, that all actions have consequences. We are shaped by and, in our turn, shape the rest of the universe.

If you search on Google for 'the good life', on UK pages only, a number of the top results refer to the 1975 BBC sitcom series with this name – still popular enough to turn up from time to time as repeats. Other results showing up on the first few pages give an interesting snapshot of what this phrase is evoking now: self-sufficiency and 'growing your own' in Britain; an orphanage in Kenya called Good Life; an article about rehabilitation in the Norwegian prison system; various publishers' announcements of books with this phrase in the title; practical advice on diet and exercise.

Amongst all these is an article from *The Independent* (8 August 2006) entitled 'The good life in Havana: Cuba's green revolution'.[4] In the 1980s, following the collapse of the Soviet empire, Fidel Castro's small island faced an oil famine and a consequent food crisis. It was a prefiguring of and laboratory for the effects of peak oil that will eventually come to us all. Today, its network of small urban farmers is thriving, an organic success story that is feeding the nation and that continues to draw the attention of green campaigners around the world.

The World Wildlife Fund (Canada) devotes a whole section of its website to The Good Life[5] – an online community of people helping each other to live more sustainable lives. A good life today has to be a version of **one-planet living**, of "living simply that others may simply live" (Mahatma Gandhi).

In the town where I live the local climate change action group recently had an interactive exhibition and discussion space in a business fair, held by and for local businesses. I spent about three hours there, helping visitors use a simple online **carbon footprint** calculator. The people who were showing low carbon emissions and coming very close to one-planet living (in carbon terms) were the poor – people unemployed or on low incomes, with whole families living in small houses, in what many of us would regard as over-crowded conditions. I was surprised at how low some of their carbon footprints were and it brought home to me yet again that, in spite of my considerable efforts to make my house carbon-efficient, the fact that I live alone has a significant impact as the carbon emissions of the house cannot be shared with other people. It was another re-minder that the environmental situation in which we find ourselves is a consequence of affluence and luxury. I don't regard my own home as luxurious, or my lifestyle as affluent – but on a global scale, they most certainly are.

> If we have food to eat, clothes to wear, a roof over our heads and a bed to sleep in, we are better off than 75 per cent of people on the planet.[6]

We have become accustomed to thinking about peak oil and our carbon footprints, but these are only a beginning. Perhaps we should next give our attention to peak water and our **water footprints**. Water use is growing twice as fast as population. Projections estimate that by 2025, two-thirds of the world population could be living in water-scarce regions, and that these water-stressed areas will con-tinue to expand in subsequent decades as a result of climate change. The melting of the Himalayan snow cap (sometimes referred to as the planet's third pole) would mean the loss of water sources for seven major rivers, affecting 40 per cent of the world's population. Water contamination is also a major issue in the developing world, where every 15 seconds a child dies of a water-related illness that is preventable in 80 per cent of cases. The goods we import from water-stressed communities are, in effect, importing virtual water from those countries to our water-abundant location. You can find personal water footprint calculators online; inevitably, they are rather crude, but – as with our carbon emissions – those of us in the rich industrialised world use more than our fair share of the world's water,[7] as well as more than our fair share of carbon.

Two-thirds of Britain's water footprint comes from 'embodied' water in imported food and goods. For example, an imported apple brings with it 70 litres of virtual water; the beans for a cup of coffee bring 140 litres; a kilogram of rice, 3,400 litres; and a kilogram of beef requires a massive 15,500 litres of water. An average cotton shirt, even if you buy it from a Fair Trade company, embodies more than 2,500 litres of water. Our Victorian ancestors treated paper as a precious and scarce commodity, to the extent of sometimes writing twice (with the lines at right-angles to each other) over every side; we have become profligate with paper along with everything else – an A4 sheet of new paper embodies 10 litres of water.[8]

Beyond water, peak wood, peak food, peak phosphate and peak soil require our attention. More than half of all soil on Earth shows signs of degradation such as erosion, desertification or salination. Over 300 million hectares of former agricultural land are now too degraded to produce food, and a further 10 million hectares become degraded or damaged every year, partly through drought and flooding (increasing with climate change). Phosphate, a vital soil chemical for healthy plant growth (gardeners will know about balancing 'PKN' in the soil), is a finite and diminishing resource in its natural state. Competition for phosphate has already become fierce, and prices are rising steeply as governments around the world seek to feed growing populations. Fortunately, phosphate is recoverable, and within the foreseeable future we could see a situation where our normal expectations of recycling include human, as well as animal, manure.

Reduced availability of fossil fuels, water and good land all impact on food production. **Food insecurity** is something we will be hearing about with greater frequency and urgency. Recent campaigns about food waste will be stepped up, and we might find statutory measures being introduced. I was brought up in the 1950s by a mother who had lived through the frugalities of World War II, and I have a deep-seated gut-sense that it is morally wrong ('sinful' even) to waste food. So I find myself shocked at the figures: in Britain, collectively, we throw away 8.3 million tons of food each year, most of which could have been eaten. Of food produced within the UK, about 11 per cent is wasted, 2.7kg per person per week. Food waste, including packaging, accounts for more than 11 million tons of waste needing disposal. According to the UN Food and Agriculture Organization, in 2009 the number of undernourished people in the world topped one billion for the first time. This is clearly insane and immoral. It will have to change. Robert Watson, **DEFRA**'s chief scientific adviser at time of writing, tells us that in order to meet future food needs, by 2030 (which is very soon) we will need 50 per cent more food production, on less land, with less water, using less energy, fertiliser and pesticide . . . while not increasing **greenhouse gas** emissions.[9]

Inevitably, in the light of this we will see changes – chosen and not chosen – to our diets. Meat production and consumption is the third-ranking cause of greenhouse gas emissions, behind buildings and transportation. One commentator wondered if 'compulsory vegetarianism' would be an outcome,[10] but it would – at the moment – be a brave political leader who would even suggest this.

> That is not to suggest that we can live harmlessly, or strictly at our own expense; we depend upon other creatures and survive by their deaths. To live, we must daily break the body and shed the blood of Creation. When we do this knowingly, lovingly, skillfully, reverently, it is a sacrament. When we do it ignorantly, greedily, clumsily, destructively, it is a desecration. In such desecration we condemn ourselves to spiritual and moral loneliness, and others to want.
>
> *Wendell Berry*[11]

Our Quaker testimony to simplicity can lull us into thinking that we know all about this – but, living in a rich country, our calibration of 'simple' is a long way from the global average. When I worked in Zimbabwe in the mid 1980s (when that newly independent country still offered hope, before its descent into tyranny), we lived on a collective farm and had what we regarded as an extremely simple lifestyle. Our Zimbabwean neighbours said, "but you are rich – you have sugar and eggs." Sugar was a sign of wealth because it couldn't be grown there, so it represented an outlay of money on an imported luxury; eggs – on a farm where chickens scratched around everywhere – showed that we had sufficient to eat and so didn't have to let the egg hatch and become a chicken.

If we are to be true to our witness to simplicity, we have a long way to go. The dimension of eco-justice has not yet made its way into the mainstream public conversation about the environment, and we as Friends may need to consider how our voice should be raised on that concern. Every reduction or saving of resources that we undertake is an act of solidarity with the poorest people in the developing world.

The dimension of what we might term **generational justice** has barely been heard yet. This is a theme I shall return to in the final chapter, but suffice it to say here that those of us born in the industrialised world in the middle portion of the twentieth century have, as a generational cohort, lived with more than our fair share even of the rich world's resources.

Beyond fair shares for all people, there are now seeds of a movement to give ecosystems, the environment, other species, some kind of legal rights. In 2008, Ecuador gave constitutional rights to the natural world:

> Nature or Pachamama, where life is reproduced and exists, has the right to exist, persist, maintain and regenerate its vital cycles, structure, functions and its processes in evolution. Every person, people, community or nationality, will be able to demand the recognitions of rights for nature before the public bodies.[12]

This is an idea and movement that we will be hearing more about. An article in 2009 put the issues clearly:

If societies express their values through the laws they make, one single legal change would completely transform our understanding of the relationship between nature and humankind: giving nature rights. And that change would be our best weapon in fighting climate change because it would give nature a voice on how we regulate the earth. The idea of 'wild law' has been around since the 1960s . . . but now enacting those ideas is a matter of our survival on this planet. Laws that recognise the world as a legal person with rights and remedies that can be enforced nationally and internationally would create a duty of care towards the environment. It is strange that we have a duty of care towards our 'neighbour', but that in law nature is not considered our neighbour.[13]

As long ago as 1982, a United Nations resolution created a World Charter for Nature.[14] From its inception, Friends have had a track record of support for the work of the United Nations;[15] and in the nineteenth century, the Friends Anti-vivisection Association[16] was part of a movement to change the cultural mindset about the treatment of animals. We are reminded in *Advices & queries* 42:

Show a loving consideration for all creatures, and seek to maintain the beauty and variety of the world. Work to ensure that our increasing power over nature is used responsibly, with reverence for life.

Perhaps the movement to give inalienable legal rights to the natural world is another area in which we, as Friends, should now make our voices heard.

There are other areas where Friends have a track-record of concern and action on an issue, from which we could extrapolate to bring time-honoured concepts to bear upon the current environmental situation. For instance, arising out of our long-standing concern and work in the field of criminal justice, can we bring models of **restorative justice** into the climate change debate? In this case, the victims are both the environment itself and poor people in the parts of the world most devastated by the effects of climate change.

What would restorative climate justice look like on a global scale?

Another example would be **Responsibility to Protect** (R2P), which was discussed by Paul Lacey in his 2010 Swarthmore Lecture.[17] R2P currently focuses on preventing and halting four crimes: genocide, war crimes, crimes against humanity and ethnic cleansing; we might seek to add to this, crimes against the environment.

To make real our testimonies to truth and to simplicity in this emerging global situation, we need to reframe how we think, how we prioritise, how we make choices, how we assign values, what our motivations are and how we communicate with others. The changes required of all of us, the demands that will be made on humanity, over the next 30 to 50 years, are enormous. A few people and communities have started to grasp the magnitude of this; collectively – as nations, as political entities – we have not yet taken the first step. Beyond recycling, beyond changing our light bulbs, beyond 'doing our bit', lies the biggest challenge of humanity's entire history. This is not about guilt and not a matter for self-laceration; it requires intelligence, imagination and cooperation from everyone. For those of us starting from a faith commitment, it requires a re-orientation to the inward springs which nourish outer action. For Friends, specifically, it requires a revitalising of what testimony means – a powerful outflowing from the depths of our spiritual experience, because we are impelled, because we can do no other.

In evolutionary terms, we are a baby species – anatomically modern human beings have only been around for about 175,000 years – but already we dominate the *real* global economy. The real economy is not that of the banks and hedge funds, but that of photosynthesis: our entire life, our food, our clothing, our buildings . . . everything depends on green plants converting the energy of sunlight into biomass. Humanity in total constitutes less than one per cent of the biomass on the surface of the Earth, yet already – at our present population level, and present distribution of technology – we use up 24 per cent of all the products of photosynthesis. As well as current photosynthesis, our use of fossil fuels means that every year we are burning up the results of previous millions of years of photosynthesis: we are burning our capital as if there were no tomorrow.[18] "We have built an entire civilisation on the carbon deposits of the Jurassic age,"

says Jeremy Rifkin. "We have to change or we have to go."[19]
How do we become the change we want to see? How do we motivate ourselves and others to do what we know is needed? How do we, as a community of Friends, as a religious body, become beacons, 'patterns and examples'? Alongside members of other religious groups, we have deeply held views about the nature of human beings. We also believe that the best can be elicited from people, given love and the right circumstances. Many favourite Quaker quotations point to this:

'the evil weakening . . . and the good raised up'
(Quaker faith & practice 19.21)

'then you will come to walk cheerfully over the world, answering that of God in every one; whereby in them you may be a blessing, and make the witness of God in them to bless you'[20]

'Our life is love, and peace, and tenderness; and bearing one with another, and forgiving one another, and not laying accusations one against another; but praying one for another, and helping one another up with a tender hand'
(Quaker faith & practice 10.01)

We need to be more bold in our beliefs in the face of what can often seem to be an indifferent and cynical world. A strong tide of new research is flowing along with us, and offers us a chance to step forward. An obvious recent example is the work of Richard Wilkinson and Kate Pickett in *The spirit level*[21] and in their work with the Equality Trust. They write:

Great income inequality is the scourge of modern societies. We provide the evidence on each of eleven different health and social problems: physical health, mental health, drug abuse, education, imprisonment, obesity, social mobility, trust and community life, violence, teenage births, and child well-being. For all eleven of these health and social problems, outcomes are very substantially worse in more unequal societies.[22]

The central message of their book has been widely taken up by a significant range of people, and not only Quakers who already uphold a testimony to equality. Alongside this book, which has attracted a lot of media attention, there is a wealth of less well-known work that gives us as Friends, as people of faith, a similar message. Research in the fields of neuroscience, behavioural economics and animal behaviour combine to give all of us important messages about the nature of humanity,[23] messages that give an added dimension to some of our deeply-held religious and spiritual beliefs.

We are a deeply social species, to a degree that challenges fundamentally the Western notion of individualism. Our beliefs, habits and behaviour are shaped, far more than we can realise, by those around us – not only by our immediate family and friends, but also by their families and friends. The other side of this, of course, is that our beliefs, habits and behaviour can influence others, our immediate associates and beyond. Making changes in our own lives will cause ripples to spread outwards from ourselves. 'Witness' does have an effect.

We know that cooperation is at least as significant in our evolutionary make-up as are aggression and competition. Throughout human history (and earlier, encompassing our pre-hominid ancestors, and our nearest biological cousins among the great apes), while the aggressive and competitive individual will prevail, a group composed of cooperative individuals will prevail over a group of competitive individuals riven by in-fighting. And being sociable is good for you – strong social ties have a major beneficial effect on physical and mental well-being.

Recent research suggests that fairness and empathy are hardwired into our brains. In monkeys as well as in humans, individuals will significantly disadvantage themselves in order not to cause pain to another; among the great apes as well as among humans, food and protection will be shared beyond the family group.

Spite, however, seems to be a uniquely human trait and, surprisingly, may be essential for a successful complex society. Cooperation requiring some self-sacrifice for the good of the whole can break down if a few selfish individuals refuse to cooperate; the capacity for spite – even when disadvantaging oneself, to keep the group norms in place by punishing another – may protect the whole society from cheats. In experimental situations where interactions are repeated, when the group acts so as to punish the freeloaders, the latter stop cheating.

When we are making decisions and weighing up competing courses of action, on average, the pain of loss is felt roughly twice as much as the pleasure of gain – so we will sacrifice gain for security. We know that in close relationships it takes roughly five kind comments to compensate for one critical one; 'bad' is felt more strongly than 'good'; and we overvalue immediate gains at the cost of future expense (in both strictly financial and other ways), which tends to make long-term planning difficult. This is because losses and gains are registered in different areas of the brain. Moral decision-making is at its core largely about sympathy and empathy, which are very complex in terms of brain activity. Some individuals seem to have more active 'sympathetic regions' in the brain, and they are more likely to act generously in the kinds of altruism/spite experiments alluded to above. Being better able to imagine the feelings and responses of others leads to behaving in a more fair and equitable manner.

Degrees of 'happiness', as reported subjectively by individuals, correlate to specific brain activity that may be objectively measured. So we can measure some aspects of how social or economic factors impact on happiness. This shows us that happiness at greater material wealth rapidly becomes the new norm, and ceases to make us happy, creating an addictive spiral of acquisition. Our *relative* wealth or poverty matters more to us than the absolute amount. Brain imaging also shows that, in people acting generously or cooperatively, the pleasure areas of the brain are activated before people know the outcome of their actions – in other words, we cooperate with others because it makes us feel good. It turns out that virtue really is its own reward. It is important to note that this instance is not about reciprocal altruism; it is something beyond that, lying at the root of what might lead us to help strangers, even at inconvenience or risk to ourselves.

These social characteristics and attitudes tell us something important about how we can help to motivate desirable change in society. An interesting example is the fine/fee issue. A fine is an expression of social disapproval of an individual's action. Its effectiveness depends not only on the financial penalty, but on the individual concerned accepting and acknowledging that she or he has transgressed in some way. If the latter dimension is absent, the financial penalty becomes ineffective as a deterrent to the socially unwanted behaviour. A real-world example of this shows up in a study of an Israeli childcare centre. Parents persistently arrived late to collect their children, forcing staff to stay well beyond the contractual closing time. A fine was introduced . . . and late parental arrivals *increased*. The parents just paid up, treating the fine as a fee that entitled them to behave according to their own convenience. They no longer felt any guilt or shame at keeping the staff late, as by reframing the fine as a fee, they absolved themselves from any moral disapproval.[24]

The distinction between fine and fee has great relevance to the question of carbon emissions. If we rely on 'the polluter pays' principle to create financial incentives to reduce carbon emissions, we risk a similar reframing: "I've paid my whack, I'm entitled to my emissions." Any moral imperative, any idea of living a good life, any sense of being a contributing member of society, vanishes in the marketisation of our morality.

There are two factors in all of this that bear upon the 'good life'. The first is that empathic, cooperative, fair-dealing traits are not superficial aspects of human behaviour, not merely a thin skin of civilisation – they are embedded in our evolutionary past and in our biology. This means that the spiritual perception and religious world-view are not 'soft' models that can easily be swept away by antagonistic political or economic ideologies. These traits can of course be overridden or distorted beyond recognition by adverse circumstances – human beings are highly malleable and adaptable – but it does mean that timeless spiritual and religious values have a new foothold in the secular world.

Secondly, the embeddedness of these traits in us also points to a framework within which to approach the changes we all need to make to the way we live: we must appeal to the best in people, in ourselves and others. To proceed by scaring ourselves and everyone else will create only paralysis, resentment or denial. To go forward using the best of what humanity can be, expecting the best of ourselves and everyone else, leading by example in a confident and cheerful manner, has the backing of science as well as spirituality.

Considering our motivation to act now so as to care for future generations, philosopher Dieter Birnbacher[25] writes of the challenge to motivate people not only to accept responsibility in the abstract, but also to internalise and adopt it as part of their deeper moral identity, so that we do the right thing because it is the right thing to do, because we are the kind of people who do that kind of thing. It might be seen as the philosopher's version of the prayer of St Ignatius:

Teach us, good Lord, to serve thee as thou deservest; to give and not to count the cost; to fight and not to heed the wounds; to toil and not to seek for rest; to labour and not to ask for any reward, save that of knowing that we do thy will.

As a child raised in the Anglican church, this prayer always felt to me to be rather grimly worthy, with no visible joy. It does not have to be like that, and I am sure that it is in part George Fox's 'cheerfulness' that has endeared to us one particular version of a good life:

This is the word of the Lord God to you all, a charge to you all in the presence of the living God; be patterns, be examples in all countries, places, islands, nations, wherever you come; that your life and conduct may preach among all sorts of people, and to them. Then you will come to walk cheerfully over the world, answering that of God in every one; whereby in them ye may be a blessing, and make the witness of God in them to bless you: then to the Lord God you shall be a sweet savour, and a blessing.[26]

Our good life will flow out of our love of life, our compassion, our joy, and then it will also touch others. If we love the Earth, we reduce our consumption and our waste because it is a truly joyful thing to do, not just a grim, guilty necessity. A good life cannot be for ourselves alone, but flows out of a love that embraces the whole of life on Earth – past, present and imagined future.

CHAPTER 4

How long is 'sustainable'?

"It is too early to say"

Zhou Enlai (first Premier of the People's Republic of China,
serving from October 1949 until his death in January 1976)
asked for his assessment of the 1789 French Revolution

Anyone who grew up in a church or school where hymn-singing was the norm will almost certainly remember 'Oh, God our help in ages past', with the lines:

A thousand ages in Thy sight
Are like an evening gone;
Short as the watch that ends the night
Before the rising sun.

These words were written by Isaac Watts in 1719 but were based on words from Psalm 90, so the sentiment expressed is perhaps 2,500 years old – long before modern geological sciences (less than 250 years old) started to give us an inkling of the true age of the Earth, now estimated to be about 4.5 billion years. Without the scientific knowledge, the intuition was nevertheless correct. On God's time-scale we are less than mayflies, ephemeral, and with a chronically short attention span.

Cosmologist Brian Swimme said:

It's really simple. Here's the whole story in one line. This is the greatest discovery of the scientific enterprise: You take hydrogen gas, and you leave it alone, and it turns into rose-bushes, giraffes, and humans.[1]

The point is that you leave it alone for a very, very, very long time. We have great difficulty imagining even much shorter time-spans than this. Quaker sociologist Elise Boulding suggested that we should expand our time horizons by thinking from our grandparents' births to our grandchildren's deaths. This would give us about 200 years – "the 200-year present"[2] – to which we can feel connected. I'm not entirely convinced about this; my grandmother's childhood was in the 1880s, and that isn't truly 'real' to me; my god-grandchildren's late adulthood will be approaching the end of this century – who can really imagine, in present circumstances, what that will be like? But we have to try. If the human habitation of this Earth is to become sustainable in reality, we have to use our imaginations and expand our time horizons; we have to believe that the distant future will be real, and act in such a way that it will be bio-friendly, not merely superficially people-friendly in the short term.

A couple of years ago I chanced, halfway through, upon someone telling a story on the radio about an Oxbridge college founded in the 1300s. The great dining hall was built with enormous oak beams, and in the late 1800s beetles were discovered in these beams. Dismay ensued – no one knew where they'd find so many oak trees big enough to replace the lost beams. Someone thought to summon the college forester and ask him if there was any oak available. It turned out that a stand had been planted and set aside when the great hall was built, and while everyone at the college had forgotten about them, the forestry people had been under strict orders, passed down for 500 years, that these oaks were not to be touched until such time as they were needed to replace the roof. The story was told as an example of appropriate long-term thinking, genuine sustainability. Because of the faith of the builders that their college would still be standing and in use hundreds of years hence, proper provision was made.

What an inspiring tale! And, being concerned about sustainability, I set about searching out the details and origins of the story. It turns out to be about New College, Oxford; and it turns out to be a fable, denied clearly and in detail by the college itself. Architect Ed van Hinte[3] comments, "the story is an embroidery on the theme of continuity and foresight which, when examined in detail, is nonsense." In spite of these clear denials, the story continues to circulate in print, electronic and broadcast media. It is attributed to psychologist Gregory Bateson, retold by Stewart Brand (of whom we shall hear more later), and the person I heard on the radio repeated it in good faith.

In similar vein, the engaging tale *The man who planted trees* tells the story of one shepherd's long and successful singlehanded effort to reforest a desolate valley in the foothills of the Alps through the first half of the twentieth century.[4] The author, Jean Giono, enjoyed allowing people to believe that the events were true, and considered it a tribute to his skill as a storyteller. In fact it is a fable, and others have come forward with similar tales in other parts of the world. However, in 1957 Giono wrote "Sorry to disappoint you. The goal was to make trees likeable, or more specifically, make planting trees likeable."[5]

In both these instances, I believe, the tenacity of the stories and of the belief in their veracity is because we *want* them to be true – in some way they 'ought' to be true. It is no coincidence that these tenacious stories are about trees; nor that, when Tolkein was writing *The Lord of the Rings*, he made trees into the Ents – ancient and wise creatures derived from many old mythological folk-tales of talking trees that are helpful to people. Ancient trees connect us back in time beyond mere human lifespans. In a small village in Perthshire there is a yew tree at least 3,000 and possibly as much as 5,000 years old. The oldest known giant sequoia in California was estimated (based on counting rings) to be 3,200 years old. These trees were alive in what we now call the Iron Age.

In 1998/99, as the millennium approached, there was a public consultation in Britain to discover what people felt would be appropriate commemorative projects. I wrote in, without much optimism, saying: "plant trees, lots of them, native broadleaf trees – re-create the English forest." I was not alone, as it turned out. There was an overwhelming surge of public support for tree planting, resulting in projects of all sizes, from central government initiatives to the fictional "millennium wood" in Ambridge (in Radio 4's *The Archers* series) that represents all the real-life small-scale local initiatives. To plant a tree is to believe in a future, maybe 100, maybe 1,000 years hence. To plant a tree is to be hopeful, not in the sense of casual optimism but of hope as an act of will, choosing a certain attitude to the future.

Trees can tell us something about that vexed term 'sustainability'. It is an abstract word, difficult to get a grip on in ways that make it mean something real. But it is actually quite simple: if we all carry on doing what we're doing now, for ever, will that work? Of course it won't, but to make 'for ever' real to us, we need to enlarge our sense of time. Trees help us to begin to do that. We need images to help us comprehend these long timescales, and images of the long past may help us imagine the long future.

BBC science presenter Michael Mosley offers us this image: imagine the age of Earth being represented by the distance from your shoulder to your fingertip. The whole of human history, back to our earliest hunter-gatherer forebears, is equivalent to the dust produced by one swipe of a nail file across your fingernail.

Geologist Jan Zalasiewicz suggests:

> Make your way to the lip of the Grand Canyon, and gaze down. In that mile-deep chasm, the strata span 1.5 billion years. Measured on such a scale, our own species would fit into a layer just three inches thick, while our industrial record should be confined to just one-hundredth of an inch.[6]

But of course, due to the constant movement of the Earth's crust, the Grand Canyon itself is not really very old in Earth terms. At the beginning of *The dragons of Eden*,[7] astrophysicist Carl Sagan gives us a much larger sense of time by mapping the history of the whole universe, not just the Earth, onto the length of one calendar year, then showing where in that year various significant events fall. The Big Bang, the origin of the universe, happens a fraction of a second after midnight, in the first moments of 1 January of this imagined year.

From our human point of view, nothing much happens for nine months, until on 9 September the solar system starts to form, and on 14 September the earliest single-celled forms of life appear on Earth. Again from the human perspective, the next significant event isn't until 1 December, when the Earth's atmosphere starts to change to a higher oxygen content. After this, it's mid-December before the first worms, the first plankton in the oceans, and the first primitive fish start to appear. Plants first start to colonise the land on 20 December, and animals on 21 December. The dinosaurs don't appear until Christmas Eve, and they become extinct on 28 December. The giant mammals flourish around 30 December, and the first humans appear around 10.30pm on 31 December, with widespread use of stone tools occurring at 11pm.

All of human history is squeezed into this last hour and a half. Fire is domesticated at around a quarter to midnight, and at four minutes to midnight our early human ancestors faced the start of the most recent ice age. The famous European cave paintings at Lascaux date to one minute before midnight. Agriculture is invented 40 seconds before midnight, with Neolithic civilisation and the earliest cities appearing 15 seconds later.

Seven seconds before midnight is the Bronze Age and the invention of the compass; six seconds gives us the Iron Age and the Kingdom of Israel. The birth of Buddha comes at five seconds, and that of Jesus at four seconds, along with the Roman Empire and Euclidean geometry. At three seconds we find the fall of Rome and the expansion of Islam, and at two seconds the Crusades. One second before midnight we have the European Renaissance, the emergence of experimental scientific method and the voyages of discovery, exploring outwards from both Europe and Ming-Dynasty China.

And squeezed into that final second is the widespread development of science and technology; the emergence of global culture; human acquisition of the means of complete self-destruction; the first steps in space exploration; and human-induced climate change.

Carl Sagan comments:

> The construction of such calendars is inevitably humbling . . . because I have arranged it that way, the first cosmic year has just ended. And despite the insignificance of the instant we have so far occupied in cosmic time, it is clear that what happens on and near Earth at the beginning of the second cosmic year will depend very much on the scientific wisdom and the distinctly human sensitivity of mankind.[8]

So the focus now shifts to the future.[9] Sagan's time-chart takes a year to bring us to midnight on 31 December, but what of 1 January, the new imagined year about to start, the future which begins with human industrialisation?

The term Anthropocene has started to gain currency to describe the most recent epoch in the Earth's geological history. It has no precise start date, but may be considered to begin sometime in the mid eighteenth century, when the activities of humans first began to have a significant global impact on the Earth's climate and ecosystems. This coincides with James Watt's invention of the steam engine in 1748. The term was coined in the year 2000 by Paul Crutzen, Nobel

Prize-winning atmospheric chemist, who regards the influence of human behaviour on the Earth in recent centuries as being significant enough to constitute a new geological era.

There is an irony for Friends in pinpointing the Industrial Revolution as the start of this process:

> [Abraham Darby's] new coke furnaces could produce molten iron to make enough pots for everybody in England. Anything at all could be made simply and in quantity. Iron became the plastic of the age . . . Where once a village craftsman had made a couple of pots a year, Darby's foundry was now producing thousands . . . He had taken the first step on Britain's road to the consumer world. Every manufactured object, anything turned out in bulk in a factory, anything made repetitively and sold in quantity, every consumer object, has its origins, in part, with the good Quaker of Coalbrookdale.[10]

So, as we turn to look to the future, we start from where we are now – a physical and social world that has already been deeply shaped by the forces of industrialisation, mechanisation, mass production and consumption; but also a social world in which the real costs of this trajectory are only now beginning to be understood.

Stewart Brand, whom I mentioned earlier, is perhaps most well-known as the originator of the *Whole Earth Catalog* in 1968. This was both an outcome of and a contributor to the counter-culture in North America in the late 1960s and early 1970s. It was published annually from 1968 to 1972 and occasionally thereafter, with a special anticipatory millennium edition appearing in 1994. The *Catalog* was a compendium of information on anything to assist with a counter-cultural, self-sufficient lifestyle. It listed tools and items that could be purchased, articles on social and community processes, advice on building and making things; Steve Jobs (of Apple Inc.) described the *Catalog* as the conceptual forerunner of the World Wide Web.

Brand – a combination of the visionary and the practical activist – is now putting his energies into a project about "time and responsibility",[11] addressing humanity's "pathologically short attention span". In 1966, before his work on the *Catalog*, he started a public campaign to have NASA release a satellite photo, rumoured to exist, of the sphere of the Earth seen from space, the first ever image of the 'Whole Earth'. He believed that such an image could become a powerful symbol, creating a sense of common destiny for all people on Earth.

His new project wants to do the same thing for time. He imagines a clock that "ticks once a year, bongs once a century, and the cuckoo comes out every millennium", embodying "deep time"[12] (by analogy with "deep space"). The Long Now Foundation[13] was set up in the period approaching the millennium, when there was a palpable sense of something coming to an end. One of the devices Brand uses in his book, to shift our thinking, is to write the years either side of the millennium as 01999 and 02000. So this book you are reading now is published in the year 02011. The Long Now Foundation, says its website,

> was established in 01996 to develop the Clock and Library projects, as well as to become the seed of a very long-term cultural institution. The Long Now Foundation hopes to provide a counterpoint to today's 'faster/cheaper' mind set and promote 'slower/better' thinking. We hope to creatively foster responsibility in the framework of the next 10,000 years.

The idea of a 'long now' is to restore both a human-scale and cosmological sense of 'now', rather than the accelerated, technology-driven, fragmented sense of 'now' that is currently so pervasive. In geological terms, 'now' is a million years or so – a mere geological eye-blink. The idea of "the 10,000 year clock" is that:

> such a clock, if sufficiently impressive and well-engineered, would embody deep time for people. It should be charismatic to visit, interesting to think about, and famous enough to become iconic in the public discourse. Ideally, it would do for thinking about time what the photographs of Earth from space have done for thinking about the environment. Such icons reframe the way people think.[14]

Ten thousand years was chosen as the time frame because it is approximately the length of time that humans have had a stable climate and technological progression – since we emerged from the last ice age. The hope is, eventually, to construct such a clock on a massive scale, so large that visitors in large numbers can walk around inside it. In the meantime, small-scale prototypes are being developed. The first prototype, completed on New Year's Eve 01999, is now in the Science Museum in London – London being chosen as the location for the first prototype because of the Greenwich Meridian.

The clock is in the Making the Modern World gallery.[15] You can go and see it now – it's about two metres tall, and has one of its dials showing the millennia. This dial makes visual sense of the current year being written as 02011 – far from being near an end, we have barely started. Imagine the year 12011, or 22011 . . . or 92011.

The 10,000-year Library provides content to go along with the long-term context provided by the clock:

> a library of the deep future, for the deep future. In a sense every library is part of the 10,000-year Library, so Long Now is developing tools . . . that may provide inspiration and utility to the whole community of librarians and archivists.

A long-term store of vital human knowledge, that will not become inaccessible as technology changes, is crucial to our future – how many people still have equipment to read information stored on 5¼-inch floppy discs?

These long-term frameworks are necessary to help us shift our perspective on our current problems and challenges. Just as our bodies are made up of the remnants of ancient exploding stars, **deep ecologist** John Seed reminds us that we are also "part of the rainforest recently emerged into thinking", and:

> Remember our childhood as minerals, as lava, as rocks? Rocks contain the potentiality to weave themselves into such stuff as this. We are the rocks dancing.[16]

Extraordinarily – or maybe not so extraordinarily – recent research[17] suggests that porous rocks might well have been the cradle of life that sheltered and enabled the development of the earliest single-celled organisms. Follow the path of evolution through time, and it turns out that we may indeed be "the rocks dancing", in more ways than John Seed could have imagined back in the 1980s.

So, with this long-term perspective in our minds (and hearts) let us now return to some of the time-tagged issues that face us today. A series of the predictions and warnings about climate change come with deadlines that tell us:

- 02020 is the latest date at which fossil fuel use must peak if we are to restrain global temperature increases to 2°C
- 02030 is the date by which we will need to produce 50 per cent more food, demanding – on the current system – 50 per cent more energy and 30 per cent more water, which we won't have
- 02040 is the current estimate of the date after which it will be too late to prevent the complete melting of the Greenland ice sheet, unless we reverse current trends immediately
- 02050 is the date by which we will see significant devastation by heatwaves and flooding[18] if we fail the 02020 deadline
- the end of the century is the date when we will experience a rise in sea-level of 1.5m or more if we fail the 02020 deadline.

In comparison with the timescales we have been looking at, these are nothing; these are a split-second 'now' in terms of the 10,000-year clock – so how do we start to let our current actions and decisions be influenced by our enlarged perspective?

To put it on a human scale:

- for members of the post-war baby boom generation, with adult children now starting to have children themselves, 02050 will be your grandchildren's middle age; the end of the century will be your great-grandchildren's old age
- for younger people, now of childbearing age, 02050 will be the beginnings of your old age, your children's middle age and your grandchildren's infancy; the end of the century will be your grandchildren's middle age.

Early Friends believed they were living in the end times, that the Second Coming would occur in their lifetimes. Everything about how to live, about choices and priorities, was shaped by this. As time went by and it became clear that this was not happening, there began a slow adaptation to living in the 'meantime'.[19] For Friends today who mourn the loss of that early radical vision, the move to living in the meantime is often perceived as a regrettable succession of accommodations and capitulations to the secular world. But, as an old cartoon has it: "The end is not nigh – you must learn to cope!"[20]

The present environmental crisis is often portrayed in apocalyptic terms – is humanity facing another kind of end time? What kind of spiritual response to this kind of time is required of us? I think we need a combination of 'now' and 'for ever' (or eternity, if you like): like the old country saying, "Live your life as if you'll die tomorrow; farm your land as if you'll live for ever."[21]

The greatest barrier to making effective changes in our behaviour towards a more sustainable way of living is the force of habit – the extraordinary proportion of our lives that are run by our autopilot. Buddhism teaches that our habitual way of existing is like being asleep, and we need to wake up; the practice of mindfulness is the way to this, together with the cultivation of compassion. And we can treat everything as mindfulness practice, whilst also practising sustainability – which is in itself an exercise in compassion for the biosphere, including ourselves and future generations.

There are three ways in which the noun 'practice' is used in English: (1) custom or habit – as in "it is my practice to go for a run every day"; (2) repetition or rehearsal – as in "I do my piano practice every day"; and (3) the specific Buddhist usage where meditation and mindfulness practice are referred to just as "practice", in an interesting usage which also includes the previous two meanings.

If you seek to practise mindfulness or awareness, then everything, every action, every moment, every situation can be regarded as an occasion of practice. For some time, I have been developing a practice (first usage, and aspiring to be the third) of treating disruptions to normal life as practice (second usage, and aspiring to be the third) for a future affected by economic decline, climate change and peak oil. Assuming that our governments aren't going to take sufficient action sufficiently quickly, we are all going to face failures of our infrastructure and interruptions to our normal supplies of energy, food, goods and services. So, when temporary glitches cause this to happen now, treat it as practice of the second type, a rehearsal (get used to the idea, get used to handling it and being resourceful) and third type (a personal mental discipline leading to equanimity in the face of irritations or worse).

There are many opportunities for this kind of practice. When my local post office was closed it caused considerable inconvenience. I had done my bit in the campaign to keep it open – this isn't in any way an argument for passivity or political/community disengagement – but when the closure happened, I thought: lots of things are going to close or disappear or reduce the service offered; *treat this as practice*.

When I fell and fractured my wrist, I had six weeks being unable to drive. I try to minimise my driving, and use public transport wherever I can, but the state of public transport where I live means that some things I need to do are not possible without a car. However, I discovered bus routes I didn't know existed and, consequently, I now know that some things I thought I had to do by car can, in fact, be done by bus; they take three or four times as long and are much less convenient; *treat this as practice*.

This is practice for many things: I may at some point in the future become permanently unable to drive for some reason; I hope to be able to give up my car completely when I retire from paid employment; the price or shortage of fuel will at some point make driving absurd anyway – even more absurd, if that's imaginable, than it is now in the face of climate change.

Then there was the ash from the Icelandic volcano in spring 02010. We can't fly? *Treat it as practice*. I know this is relatively easy for me – I haven't been on a long-haul flight since 01985 or a short-haul one since 01987. I don't have a life that depends on flying, I don't have family living abroad and very few of my friends live outside western Europe. But even if you do have a life that depends on flying, do have family living abroad and do have friends all over the world, you can't assume that you will always be able to jump on a cheap flight to see them. This is going to change, either gradually or, more likely, suddenly. It could be fuel prices that do it, or fuel shortages, or another, bigger and more dangerous volcano. Regard this one as practice; and if you weren't personally caught up in it this time, treat it as a thought-experiment for practice.

For all the changes ahead of us, we need to be prepared, we need to be practised; and the practice we need is spiritual, psychological, emotional and very, very practical.

CHAPTER 5

We are all crew

And I heard the voice of the Lord saying,
"Whom shall I send, and who will go for us?"
Then I said, "Here I am! Send me."

Isaiah 6:8 (ESV)

There are no passengers on Spaceship Earth.
We are all crew.

Marshall McLuhan

What is the fundamental difference between passengers and crew? In a crisis the crew are "all hands on deck" while passengers typically stand in frightened huddles, waiting to be told what to do or else fighting over what they perceive as inadequate resources for safety and survival. In addition the crew know how to fix things that go wrong and mend things that are broken. They work as a team and act purposefully.

In the current environmental crisis – I do not say "coming crisis" because it is with us already – there is no space for passengers: we all have to take responsibility. And if we are all crew, then we all need to be well-informed and trained; just as, among unprogrammed Friends, our commitment to the priesthood of all believers means that we each have to offer gifts, talents, ministry in many forms, leadership and seriousness of purpose. Indeed, the founding of Woodbrooke was based on this realisation: if we are all to be priests, then we all need to be trained:

> There must be means placed in the reach of any Friend, who feels the call to the ministry, for still further equipment, and for closer study.[1]

So what is needed to turn passengers into crew?

There is a substantial field of research into human behaviour that goes under the name of 'bystander intervention' or 'bystander apathy'; whilst none of us has the luxury of being bystanders on the Earth at the present moment, this work is nevertheless very instructive for our current situation. And it is by no means of merely recent interest, as a 2,000-year-old story makes clear:

> A man was going down from Jerusalem to Jericho, and he fell among robbers, who stripped him and beat him, and departed, leaving him half dead. Now by chance a priest was going down that road; and when he saw him he passed by on the

other side. So likewise a Levite, when he came to the place and saw him, passed by on the other side. But a Samaritan, as he journeyed, came to where he was; and when he saw him, he had compassion, and went to him and bound up his wounds, pouring on oil and wine; then he set him on his own beast and brought him to an inn, and took care of him. And the next day he took out two denarii and gave them to the innkeeper, saying, "Take care of him; and whatever more you spend, I will repay you when I come back."

Luke 10:30–35 (RSV)

Modern research[2] on bystander behaviour began after an incident in the USA that shocked the public and became a matter of serious national debate and soul-searching. This was the murder of Kitty Genovese in 1964, when 38 neighbours watched and listened but did not act to help and did not call the police.[3] However, the neighbours' reactions were not much different from those in other emergency situations where people "watch the drama in helpless fascination". Why do people, who are so willing to help in non-emergency situations, not offer help in emergencies?

First, there are few positive rewards in an emergency. Life may be threatened for both the victims and the helpers. Secondly, since an emergency is by definition an unusual event, reactions are untrained and unrehearsed. An emergency comes without warning and so there are no practised responses to fall back on, yet it requires instant action, putting the potential helper under a lot of stress. Research in many situations has demonstrated that when someone happens upon an ambiguous or unfamiliar situation, the person may look to others' behaviours to see if they observe it as an emergency. An individual, seeing the inaction of others, will judge the situation as less serious than if that person were alone.

A potential intervener must make a series of five decisions: notice the event and interpret it as an emergency; decide if s/he has a responsibility to act; if so, decide what form the assistance should take; decide whether help should be offered directly or the emergency services be called; decide how to act and implement their choice.

More recent detailed research[4] has uncovered the many factors that influence people's willingness to help in a situation they find themselves in:

- In ambiguous situations (where it is unclear if there is an emergency), people are much less likely to offer assistance than in situations involving a clear-cut emergency; they are also less likely to help in unfamiliar environments than in familiar ones.
- The likelihood of helping increases as the perceived personal cost (time, money, inconvenience) to ourselves declines.
- The presence of others may diffuse and diminish the sense of individual responsibility.
- People are more willing to help others whom they perceive to be similar to themselves (in dress, appearance, ethnicity, etc.)
- People are generally more willing to help others when they are in a good mood.
- Women in need are more likely than men in need to receive assistance from strangers.
- People are much more likely to help others they judge to be 'innocent victims' than those they believe have brought their problems on themselves.

This research applies to emergencies, and although the current environmental crisis actually is an emergency, it is a "long emergency"[5], which makes it hard for most people to perceive it as such.

Our biological nature predisposes us to certain kinds of reactions and responses – the default modes to which we will revert without firm intention and vigilance. Hardwired into our brains, from deep in our evolutionary past, are two systems of responses: System A (emotion/gut); and System B (reason/head). System B works slowly, weighs up the evidence, calculates, considers and can explain; System A is outside conscious awareness, is very fast, makes snap judgements and relies on 'hunches'. These two brain systems both work all the time on all life issues, not always accurately. 'Gut' is the stone-age system and is not at all adapted to modern living – it still lives the pre- or early-hominid life of the African savannah. 'Gut' is great with stories and hopeless with statistics.[6]

A good example, illustrating the differences between the two systems, is provided by the two major recent climate change films, *An inconvenient truth*[7] and *The age of stupid*.[8] The first of these, Al Gore's film based on his own lectures and featuring himself – a well-known politician – is relentlessly logical, rational and full of statistics and graphs, setting out the facts as clearly as it can in the hope of persuading our thinking. The second, Franny Armstrong's more recent film, employs a well-known and loved actor, Pete Postlethwaite, and tells a story. It uses anecdote, real-life interviews, fantasy and powerful images appealing to our emotions. I was a scientist originally and my personal preference is Al Gore's approach, but it was Franny Armstrong and her film that produced the **10:10 campaign** – which had all our main political parties signing up within 48 hours of its launch, each of them judging that they could not be seen not to be supporting it.

But there is a serious problem with relying wholly on tugging at the heartstrings or pressing the fear buttons. In an American study,[9] in which people were played recordings of actors delivering speeches about climate change, the version that people responded to most positively talked about "air pollution" rather than "climate change". Pollution is something visible that they could relate to, carrying implications of dirtiness and poor health. Climate change is, of course, about much more than dirty air, but finding ways of making climate change more visible is critical. Most people simply are not going to worry about things they can neither see nor imagine.

Another piece of research, conducted in Canada,[10] presents an apparent paradox when it comes to sustainability. Polls indicate that Canadians are among the most staunchly pro-environment citizens on the planet. Yet their actions often do not live up to their words. The attitudes and values of participants in this research in support of sustainability were clear, consistent and strongly held from the outset. The gap between stated values and behaviour was the result of a set of practical barriers, which participants were able to identify and discuss in some detail.

The researchers uncovered six barriers to people acting more sustainably. First there are *structural barriers* – making sustainable choices often feels like swimming upstream, and sustainable alternatives cost more and are less convenient. Secondly, there are *mindset barriers* – there are internal expectations and assumptions that often get in the way: force of habit; consumerism; a sense of material entitlement; believing that one person cannot make a difference; feeling that environmentalism means deprivation; fatalism. Thirdly, there are *barriers of information and communication* – there is a lack of reliable information and feedback: prices for goods and services do not reflect real environmental costs; product labels do not provide reliable information; quality assessments tend to reinforce short-term economic factors; media coverage of sustainability looks at short-term, isolated stories, diminishing a sense of urgency and reinforcing the sense that it's all too complex for individual action to have any effect.

The fourth barrier is about *trust* (or, more accurately, *mistrust*), and this emerged as the most fundamental barrier to effective action on sustainability values. When citizens believe that others, especially political or corporate leaders, cannot be trusted to do their fair share, they are less likely to take action themselves. The fifth barrier was a sense of *isolation* – a weak sense of community and engagement. Participants said that without a stronger sense of community and engagement it would be more difficult, if not impossible, to build trust or move toward effective shared action on sustainability.

The final barrier was *the term 'sustainability' itself*. Participants felt that the term was too abstract, too far removed from the practicalities of everyday life, and that it tended to reinforce the idea that the problem was overwhelming and alienating. Several added that 'sustainability' seemed little more than a buzz word for bureaucrats and technical experts, one that meant different things to different people.

Although this research was undertaken in the specifics of the Canadian situation, the outcomes are recognisable as issues that we also face in Britain. And it is immediately clear that these findings correlate with what was described earlier about bystanders responding (or not) to events they encounter: our beliefs about a situation, what we believe about ourselves and other people, the information we have available to us – all impact on our willingness and ability to act. In terms of how our brain systems process information about the world around us, there is a real problem for climate and other environmental scientists in how to combine accuracy and proper scientific caution about research results with the stories and memorable images that the media and brain System A need.

So where can we look for models or examples to help us think about this extended emergency that we are in? Where can we find examples of people transforming themselves from passengers into crew?

There is an organisation called The Jewish Foundation for Christian Rescuers,[11] founded by Eva Fogelman, the daughter of a Holocaust survivor who owed his life to the intervention of his Russian employer.[12] Fogelman sought out and interviewed people who had rescued Jews, wanting to discover what predisposes some people to resist social pressures to condone oppression and evil in terrible situations when the majority are unable to do so. She links the rescuers (conceptually, spiritually, and theologically) to the Talmudic tradition of the *Lamed Vav*, the 36 people in each generation who, unknown to themselves or others, are the "righteous among the nations of the world".[13]

The rescuers never thought of themselves as heroic, and many were telling their stories for the first time. Many were psychically wounded because the relationship with the person they rescued was severed and they did not know whether that person had actually survived or not. All felt that they had not done enough – when they reached their limit they felt they had failed. All were reluctant to be given special attention. None saw themselves as morally courageous. All were ordinary, imperfect people.

Fogelman asked what turns a bystander into a rescuer and used the five steps from bystander research to analyse the stories she was told. In addition, she focussed on:

> *Awareness*: the rescuers saw what others did not, penetrating the propaganda; they often had an extra sensitivity because of the death of someone close to them; sometimes they were jolted into awareness by a transforming encounter, sometimes by an accumulation of events over time.

> *Assuming responsibility*: rescuers believed strongly that what you do or fail to do matters a great deal; they seldom had time for thought and most did not initiate the rescue – they re-

sponded to a request for help; a "rescuer self" then emerged; they felt better about themselves for acting but often felt unable to live up to this again during the rest of their lives.

Fogelman uncovered several motivational and background factors in her research:

Morality: the rescuers had a clear sense of right and wrong that was not dependent on the approval of others; they had a strong need to maintain their own integrity; they were mostly not activists but had strong ethical beliefs; in their religious beliefs, they relied on their own faith, not on church leadership, often feeling cut off from their church; they felt strong compassion for victims.

Closeness to despised group: many had love, friendship, family connections or childhood friends who were Jews; this created an affinity so that they saw Jews as known and familiar, not alien.

Concerned professionals: some were motivated by more detached or emotionally distant professional concerns; the rescue was part of a professional ethic.

Belonging to a network: some rescuers were affiliated to political or other groups opposed to Nazi ideology; these people were activists and strongly bonded to their group.

Family rescuers: these had been children who gradually became aware of their parents' activities and were drawn in, later taking over responsibility.

So, although these rescuers had responded in the moment to a need when it presented itself to them, their actions had not come out of nowhere but had been nurtured over a lifetime of choosing to live a certain way. They had, we might say, been preparing all their lives to be crew. As Iris Murdoch observes, the moral life is not something that is switched on at a particular crisis, but is something that goes on continually in the small piecemeal habits of living: "at crucial moments of choice most of the business of choosing is already over."[14]

This echoes Aristotle, who wrote that we acquire our virtues by a process of habituation; in order to become a better person, the first thing to do is act like a better person: walk in the shoes of the person we want to become. Act it out first, acquire the right habits, and our behaviour will eventually shape our characters. Commenting on this in a BBC Radio 4 Lent Talk, Giles Fraser (formerly Rector of St. Mary's, Putney; now a Canon at St. Paul's Cathedral) said:

> One of the important things about going to church a lot is that it does act a bit like a deliberate rehearsal for doing things right. The repetition of our theology in prayer and ritual and music are ways of keeping us true to what we profess to believe, shaping our affections and character, sculpting our identity so that we might be better prepared for what life might throw at us. This idea of how we might grow in moral character is not one that makes much sense to those who assume that the first thing we have to get right is how we are or how we feel inside. This common way of presenting things assumes that moral change, the development of courage or becoming more sensitive to others, for instance, is generated from the inside out. And from this perspective, the idea that you might change first by altering how you behave looks insincere, almost hypocritical. But it isn't . . . For although we can never fully know how we will behave in stressful situations, what many of the great psychologists and philosophers say . . . is that in extremis, we are the people we have practised to be.[15]

So, in both the emergency situations examined in the earlier research, and in the more drawn-out context of Fogelman's respondents, the crucial stage in the process of becoming a bystander who intervenes (turning passenger into crew) is the step of taking responsibility. What can help and enable that? What are the "small piecemeal habits of living", as Murdoch puts it, that can nurture in us a capacity to respond with what is needed? I will return to this question in the final chapter.

Let us move now to thinking about these fields of research specifically in relation to our attitudes to climate change, and apply the five steps in the 'bystander' process:

- notice that climate change is a problem
- interpret this as a situation in which something needs doing
- assume personal responsibility for doing something
- choose what to do
- implement that decision.

It is clear that climate change is a problem – it has already been noticed – and it is clear that something must be done: these are the easy steps. The critical third step is that we – each and all of us – take responsibility for doing something. This is where the Canadian research, quoted earlier, can help us. All of the reasons given were why individuals should *not* do something. There are always many available arguments for not doing something, whereas the one valid reason *for* doing something is that it is the right thing to do. And one of the common factors found among the bystanders who intervened, who assumed responsibility, was a strong belief that what you do or fail to do does actually make a difference. There are plenty of pieces of sage advice about how doing a small thing is doing something and is not doing nothing: the images of lighting candles instead of cursing the darkness and of taking the first step on a thousand-mile journey spring immediately to mind.

Perhaps more pointed, in our current situation, is James Hansen's advice. Hansen, a senior scientist in NASA, was the person who first said that the ice caps would respond quickly to **global warming**, and he was right. The stark message of his most recent book[16] may be summed up as this: the situation is worse than we are being told, "your governments are lying through their teeth", nothing is being done, you can't "compromise" with nature and the laws of physics; consequently, civil resistance may soon be the only way forward – "it is up to you". It was published before the 2009 Copenhagen climate summit, and the outcomes of that event give us nothing with which to challenge his message.

From someone in a position to know, here is a clear call for us all to start behaving like crew and not passengers. It was echoed, following the 2010 Cancún climate summit, by Gustavo Esteva, a Mexican activist and founder of the *Universidad de la Tierra* (University of the Earth) in Oaxaca, Mexico. He writes:

> In the efforts to protect our planet from ourselves, the high level talks at Cancún were our last chance . . . and they failed. But we can learn from this sad episode: we must stop asking governments and international organisations for solutions that they don't want to – and can't – implement . . . All governments, even the most majestic, are composed of ordinary mortals, trapped in bureaucratic labyrinths and fighting vested interests that tie their hands, heads and wills . . . We must look . . . to the people, and what we can do ourselves . . . The time has come to change the system, not the planet. That depends on us, not on those who gain status and income from the system.[17]

What might this mean in practical terms? Well, to start with, it means all the easy things we already know about, but may not have yet implemented in our own lives. We all know what they are: insulate our houses, use less gas and electricity, reduce our travelling and change our means of travel, eat less meat (or none at all), reduce all consumption and waste, re-use, repair and recycle everything we can, shop less and shop local, reduce food miles, 'grow your own', compost food waste, buy without packaging, cook fresh food from scratch instead of buying processed food . . . and so on. Many of us are already doing some of this, some of the time; we *all* need to do all of it, all of the time, consistently and reliably, forever. These are all decisions we can make individually or by household.

Beyond that, things start to get a bit more difficult. Consider, for instance, deciding not to fly to Australia (or wherever it is) to see the grandchildren, because flying is contributing to creating a world that will not be fit for those grandchildren to grow up in. If enough individuals or families take that decision, then the extra runway at Heathrow starts to look less attractive to the investors. But we have to take the tiny, seemingly ineffectual individual decisions first. It really does matter that each of us takes the trouble to make these personal decisions. They are not too small to make a difference – as we saw in Chapter 3, the fact that we are a social species means that individual influence has an effect on others, even if we can't see it at the time.

Many Friends have started to talk about a "testimony to the Earth" – such a testimony will emerge, grow and become real precisely to the extent that we all conduct our lives in a sustainable manner. Testimony is not a form of words but the cumulative lived witness of Friends in day-to-day life.[18] It lies in our hands – each of us separately and all of us collectively – to live in such a way that we create this testimony. If we are faithful to this calling, an Earth testimony has the potential to grow into something as significant for us (and as influential in the world) as is the peace testimony.

Beyond our private lives, how about tackling the carbon emissions of the places where we work? This might involve us in difficult conversations with management; if we are management, then it might involve us in difficult conversations with trustees or shareholders; if we are trustees or shareholders, then it's time we faced the fact that increased costs or reduced profits in the short term are not an argument for doing nothing.

And then there's our local area, the place where we live and its local government structures. Is Transition Town activity already happening? If so, are we involved? If not, can we, as Quakers, help to start it? Would it help to think of ourselves as Transition Friends or Transition Quakers?[19]

Do we know what our local councillors are doing, or not doing, about sustainability? Are they actively supporting local food initiatives and markets? Are they actively seeking land to supply more allotments and get hopeful growers off the waiting list? Can we find out, question them, make it an election issue for next time? Might a few more of us be called to take our Quaker values into the public, political arena and stand for election as local councillors?

What about our local MPs? Do we know their views? Are they

signed up to the 10:10 campaign? We can start writing letters, holding public figures to account. We can do all of this before we get anywhere near James Hansen's advised position of "civil resistance".

These are all the basic minimal things that every responsible citizen needs to do, whether or not they have any religious underpinning. For those of us who profess a faith, how can we countenance doing less?

And what about our local Quaker meetings and our meeting houses? That, too, will be looked at in the final chapter.

CHAPTER 6

The time is now

You do not have to change: survival is not mandatory

W. Edwards Deming

I have set before you life and death, blessings and curses.
Now choose life, so that you and your children may live.

Deuteronomy 30:19 (NIV)

If I am not for myself, then who will be for me?
And if I am only for myself, then what am I?
And if not now, when?

Rabbi Hillel, Ethics of the Fathers *1:14*

Where your talents and the needs of the world cross,
therein lies your vocation

Aristotle

Whatever your hand finds to do,
do it with all your might.

Ecclesiastes 9:10 (NIV)

There is a brief and memorable model of change that puts just three questions into an iterative circle:

What?

Now what?   So what?

You start by examining the actual situation, the known facts, the present circumstances; then you evaluate the significance of these and tease out the implications; lastly you decide on a course of action. This action will produce a change in the circumstances, so the cycle goes around again.

In the preceding chapters we have looked at some of 'what?' and 'so what?' and now we come inevitably to the thorny question of 'now what?'. I have already mentioned a number of campaigns and movements to which we might appropriately lend our voice and energies, but I have in mind something more fundamental than that. Action, in our Quaker context, is testimony – faith in action, witness in the world, Spirit-led ways of living because we can do no other. The point is to "bring in the Kingdom" – or "the republic of heaven" – to engage in *tikkun olam*, a Hebrew phrase meaning "repairing the world". As Karl Marx put it, "The philosophers have only interpreted the world in various ways; the point, is to change it"[1] – we find our allies wherever they may be.

Marx also said, more than 150 years ago (writing in 1858):

> For the first time, nature becomes purely an object for humankind, purely a matter of utility . . . whether as an object of consumption or as a means of production.[2]

He was ahead of his time. What he describes has come to pass in ways beyond anything he could have imagined, and the time to act is now.

For me, the crucial and underlying question for us as Quakers is: are we content to be merely a support group for people on their individual spiritual journeys, or are we able to rediscover solidarity as a people of God? The latter would of course include elements of the former, but would be something much larger and deeper, much more demanding, much more daunting and challenging. I believe we are called at this time to rediscover what this can mean.

In the reforms to the Roman Catholic monastic communities undertaken following the Second Vatican Council, one call was for them to return to their founding charism. This was emphatically not, as T. S. Eliot so eloquently put it, to "revive old factions/ . . . restore old policies/Or follow an antique drum."[3] The religious communities were charged with a process of renewal that would rediscover and reinterpret their original charism for the modern world.

What would it mean for us as the Religious Society of Friends to undertake such a task? What would the 'founding charism' of early Friends look like, reinterpreted for the twenty-first century? I don't, of course, have a simple answer to my own question – and it is not a question for one person to answer alone, but for a community to discover together.[4] But I do have some pointers to what might be involved, and they all include us moving substantially out of our various comfort zones.

My first pointer is the rediscovery (or in some cases discovery for the first time) of the importance of spiritual discipline. This matters both for its own sake (for God's sake) and as preparation for the times that are ahead of us. The point of a spiritual discipline lies in what the Buddhists call it: practice. It is practice in the same sense as training in sports, or as playing your scales and doing your five-finger exercises if you are a pianist. It is not exciting, mostly it is not interesting, often it is dull and tedious, but you do it regularly and faithfully because without it you cannot do what you deeply and truly desire to do – break that world record, play that difficult sonata. Spiritual discipline is five-finger exercises for the soul. It trains the mind and heart, the psyche and the emotions, so that when the going is tough, when the ordinary comforts are not available, when the demands on us seem to be greater than our capacity, we have something that we can rely upon. We cannot start to create this resilience when things are already difficult, any more than we could run a marathon tomorrow morning if we only started training this afternoon.

A spiritual discipline is not undertaken for utilitarian reasons in the way that a stress-management programme might be; but a spiritual discipline, sustained for intrinsic reasons, will turn out to have extrinsic benefits. What distinguishes any practice as a 'spiritual discipline' is that it takes a specific part of your way of life and turns it constantly towards the Spirit. A spiritual discipline, when practised faithfully and regularly, is a habit or regular pattern in your life that repeatedly brings you back to the spiritual centre, and opens you up to where the Spirit is leading you.

There are many forms of such discipline – traditional prayer and reflective Bible reading; reflective reading of other texts including *Quaker faith & practice*; mindfulness meditation; various body-disciplines such as yoga, t'ai chi or qigong; journal-writing, painting or other art work; mindful walking, gardening or handwork; and many others. It can also be faithfully visiting an elderly neighbour or undertaking some other form of practical service.

Turning any of these activities into a spiritual discipline involves first, *intention* – that we approach them with that purpose and desire; second, *mindfulness* – that we actively seek to sustain a focused and calm awareness of the present moment and turn away from distractions and scattered thoughts; third, that we *practise regularly* – our mind-body will soon learn that a particular time, place, or activity is for practice (in exactly the same way as we habituate an infant to bedtime), so the habit of mindfulness will grow and start to spread out into more and more of our daily life.

All such practices remove our individual egos from the centre of the stage; similarly, we – humanity – also need to find ways of moving our collective ego out of the way. If we took humans out of Earth's ecosystem, the present world would function quite happily, as it did 200,000 years ago before our species evolved; but if we took away the worms and the insects, the whole system would start to fall apart. If we took away the viruses and bacteria and their more ancient relatives, the archaea, then the world would, quite simply, die.[5] Gaia, as James Lovelock described her,[6] would cease to be. We are not the most important beings on the planet.

In addition to the three *characteristics* – intention, mindfulness, regular practice – there are some helpful *attitudes* for establishing a life-giving spiritual discipline. The first is a version of "pray as you can, not as you can't" – don't try to do something you think you ought to do if it means setting yourself up to fail; this shouldn't be like taking out gym membership on 2 January and then giving up by the end of the month! Second, find something that works for your temperament,[7] abilities and daily life – be realistic. Be gentle with yourself – don't force yourself when you're too tired; but if you're often too tired, ask yourself why that is. Lastly, consider finding a Spiritual Friend, a 'prayer buddy', a companion for your journey – you can encourage and uphold each other.

Undertaken faithfully and sustained over time, such practices attune our inner ear to the promptings of the Spirit, so that when we are called, when our service is required, we will hear the call and have the capacity to respond. This is true for each of us as individuals; it is also the case for us as local communities of Friends and as a national or world Quaker community.

Which brings me to my second pointer: are we, and in what ways are we, willing to be community with and for each other? Being community means being willing to be accountable to each other, in ways that early Friends were, and that we find much more challenging in our twenty-first-century individualistic culture. Being community, being accountable, means relinquishing some individual freedoms – and the benefits to be gained cannot become apparent to us until we have taken that step. The commitment itself starts the process of change and growth:

> Until one is committed, there is hesitancy, the chance to draw back, always ineffectiveness. Concerning all acts of initiative and creation, there is one elementary truth the ignorance of which kills countless ideas and splendid plans: that the moment one definitely commits oneself, then providence moves too. All sorts of things occur to help one that would never otherwise have occurred. A whole stream of events issues from the decision, raising in one's favour all manner of

unforeseen incidents, meetings and material assistance which no man could have dreamed would have come his way.[8]

And this leads us to my third pointer, action: "Only a demanding common task builds community."[9] The demanding task facing the whole of humanity is quite clear, even though our political leaders ducked it at the climate summit in Copenhagen in December 2009 and again in Cancún in December 2010. But what, specifically, might be our task as Quakers? Here is one possibility which may be familiar to some of you already, as I have been talking about it with various small groups of Friends for a couple of years now.

We know that it is imperative for individuals and institutions to reduce their carbon emissions, and that this is not a one-off operation but a progressive year-on-year reduction. This is known as carbon descent, and groups of people who work together to achieve this are known as **low carbon communities**. In most cases a low carbon community is a geographically proximate group of people – perhaps a village, a street, a school or other institution, a business or other similar grouping. But let us consider the possibility of a dispersed low carbon community. Of course, I have in mind Britain Yearly Meeting. What would it mean for Quakers in Britain to be truly a low carbon community?

For this possibility to become real, for it to embody our testimony to simplicity and our testimony to truthfulness, it would require a number of steps to be taken: that each of us as individual members of the yearly meeting commit ourselves honestly and practically to progressively reducing our carbon emissions by an agreed amount, year on year on year (the 10:10 campaign would make that figure 10 per cent – challenging but achievable); that each of our meetings and meeting houses does the same; that area meetings or other functions be held in a manner that reduces the carbon emissions of all that travelling; that Woodbrooke, Friends House and other Quaker-owned or Quaker-run organisations also succeed in this reduction; and that we find low-carbon methods of holding Yearly Meeting and Meeting for Sufferings.

This would require from us commitment and discipline. Our commitment would have to be not only to carbon reduction but also to the corporate witness of Quakers in Britain. The discipline required would encompass our carbon-related behaviour as well as the mutual accountability of being part of a larger corporate body. In any group of people, a balance is required to sustain the healthy functioning of that group: a balance between an inward focus, on the life and processes of the group, and an outward focus, embodying the group's *raison d'être* and relating to the wider world. Thinking of Friends, we should add also a focus on the Spirit – which is, of course, not the same thing as a focus inward on the group.

It is perhaps in the nature of Friends – in the way we worship, in the kinds of people who are attracted to the ways of Friends – that a tendency to turn inwards is very strong. When this becomes dominant, losing the balance of an outward focus, the inevitable tendency is to stagnation and loss of vital energy. Among British Friends, the Quietist period in the eighteenth century led to this kind of stagnation. Friends have been most influential and effective in our witness when tested by external circumstances – when the world presents dilemmas that require the best of Quaker spiritual discipline, both individual and corporate. In Britain, this was particularly manifest in the two world wars. Friends had a clear issue to confront, requiring steadfastness and faithfulness, and their public stance drew many people to seek out Friends for succour, spiritual nurture and practical support. For the generations alive now climate change is the testing issue of our times.

So this is potentially a moment in history when Quakers are needed – needed to be faithful to Quaker testimonies; needed to be visible, to be speaking out, to be offering leadership; needed to do what is right in the face of external pressing circumstances. To use Gandhi's phrase, Quakers – individually and corporately – need and are needed to "be the change we wish to see in the world". To do and be so will require us to deepen our spiritual grounding, alone and together – not only for the sake of inward exploration but for the future of human society. A further challenge will be to find the corporate will, the rediscovery of a depth of corporate discipline, to undertake this wholly and fully, not just as a matter of piecemeal personal choices. Our dispersed and devolved patterns of leadership, authority and decision-making add a layer of difficulty.

Other churches and faith groups, with more traditional hierarchical organisational patterns, are forging ahead in this field, in their own ways, but it remains to be discovered how far congregation members will follow their leaders.

But if we, as Friends, were to find our way to "be the change", we would not only contribute vitally to the necessary decarbonising of British society; we would not only offer a beacon of leadership to others lacking a community context; we would also strengthen, deepen and revitalise the life of our Society. Are we ready to undertake this?

What is the spirituality that we need for the planetary emergency that we now face? There is an African proverb that says "If you want to go fast, go alone; if you want to go far, go with others." But we – humanity – need to go both far and fast; we need a new consciousness, a new spirituality that can reach out to everyone. Franny Armstrong, who created the film *The age of stupid* and the 10:10 campaign, wrote:

> I was born in the '70s as part of the MTV generation who were told by a squillion adverts that the point of our existence was to shop more. Daunting though the task ahead may be, I feel enormously inspired and quite relieved that it turns out that we have something important to do. The people who came before us didn't know about climate change and the ones who come after will be powerless to stop it. So it's down to us. Other generations came together to overturn slavery or end apartheid or win the vote for women. There is nothing intrinsically more useless about our generation and there is no doubt about what we have to do. The only question which remains is whether or not we give it a go.[10]

She articulates the challenge faced by all of us alive at this time, and it reminds me of something I read many years ago:

> Here is a test to find whether your mission on earth is finished: If you're alive, it isn't.[11]

We are the people alive now, we are the people who know about the problem. Who else do we imagine is going to do what needs to be done? What we need is a consciousness and a spirituality that creates in us joy, gratitude, determination, courage and humility – in the knowledge that we are doing God's work. And we cannot do this without spiritual practices and ways of living that will sustain and nourish us over the very long haul.

First, we need to strengthen, or remake, the depth of our connectedness with the rest of creation, with the whole web of life.[12] The molecules that make up our bodies have been exchanged untold numbers of times with other parts of the natural world – at the level of physics and biology we are totally part of, and not in any way separate from, the rest of the universe. But there is more than that. The fundamental make-up of our bodies and brains – and thus of our psychology, emotions and spirituality – evolved when humans were few and far between on the Earth, when we lived embedded in a natural world not yet shaped by us and for our purposes.

Our bodies work best when we are active and spend most of our time moving about. Today we call it exercise; for our ancient ancestors, it was just living. And not only our bodies – our emotions also become more positive when we exercise: endorphins (feel-good chemicals) are released in the brain. Regular physical exercise is a good antidote to depression, something known by the monastic communities where mindfully digging the vegetable garden is as much part of the religious life as is singing in choir. But there is yet more to it than this. How many of us feel uplifted by the sight of wild animals, birds, trees in autumn colour or spring budburst, waterfalls, mountains, oceans? It has been found that hospital patients recover more quickly if they can see trees outside their windows.[13] We have evolved to respond to beauty in the natural world, and even at the molecular level, we have evolved in tandem with our surroundings. Ancient woodland[14] produces a rich mix of organic chemicals in the air and it seems that we gain very particular benefits from breathing in this arboreal cocktail: reduced heart rate and blood pressure, lowered blood-sugar levels in diabetics.[15] The Japanese have a word for this: *shinrin-yoku* or 'wood-air bathing'. Our connection with the natural world is deep, real and inescapable – we must re-own and re-value it.[16]

Remaking this heart-connection will not be without emotional cost. We may find ourselves needing to grieve the loss of species and habitats, the impoverishment of our environment and our inability to save everything. Of course we should grieve the loss of something we love, and we should not minimise the spiritual loss to humanity:

> What is man without the beasts? If all the beasts were gone, man would die from a great loneliness of the spirit. For whatever happens to the beasts, soon happens to man. All things are connected.
>
> *Attributed to Chief Seattle, chief of the Suquamis*

The *second* thing we need to do to sustain and nourish us over the long haul is to rebuild community – within our meetings, within each of our local neighbourhoods; and by integrating our meetings more deeply and broadly within the geographic communities where they happen to be located. How to do this? Here are one group's suggestions:

Turn off your TV * Leave your house * Know your neighbors
Look up when you are walking * Greet people * Sit on your stoop
Plant flowers * Use your library * Play together
Buy from local merchants * Share what you have * Help a lost dog
Take children to the park * Garden together
Support neighborhood schools * Fix it even if you didn't break it
Have pot lucks * Honor elders * Pick up litter * Read stories aloud
Dance in the street * Talk to the mail carrier * Listen to the birds
Put up a swing * Help carry something heavy
Barter for your goods * Start a tradition * Ask a question
Hire young people for odd jobs * Organize a block party
Bake extra and share * Ask for help when you need it
Open your shades * Sing together * Share your skills
Take back the night * Turn up the music * Turn down the music
Listen before you react to anger * Mediate a conflict
Seek to understand * Learn from new and uncomfortable angles
Know that no one is silent though many are not heard.
Work to change this.[17]

And here is a much shorter list:

Connect; Be active; Take notice; Keep learning; Give.[18]

The point about both of these lists is that building a community requires us all to participate, to take responsibility. It is another version of us all being crew. Community isn't something that other people create so that I, you, we can then become parasitical on it and reap the benefits. Community only happens when everyone takes part in creating it – if we want our local Quaker meetings to be more vibrant places, then none of us can be a passenger. Who else do we think is going to do this? This view of community fits so well with our ways of organising ourselves as a religious society, with no separated ministry, that we might hope we would be naturally good at this. We need to practice – in all the shades of meaning of that word discussed earlier: we need to get good at it, we need to make it habitual, and we need to make it a vital part of our corporate spiritual discipline.

The *third* change we have to make is to find new ways of framing the issues, to reclaim as well as declaim a radical vision for the future. To give one example, in the film *The age of stupid* there is a short animation sequence that illustrates the idea of **contraction and convergence** – a dreadful abstract phrase that will never inspire anyone. The animation starts by showing the current global distribution of per-capita carbon emissions represented as differently sized people:

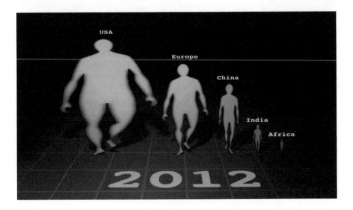

The characters then walk forwards along the timeline, gradually equalising in size:

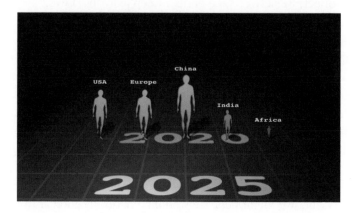

until, at the year 2035, all the characters are equal. Then as they walk forwards to 2065, they all shrink at the same rate:

This is a powerful image, not only of carbon reduction but also of global equity. Let us reclaim a powerful political word for this: levelling. The English Levellers of the seventeenth century did not actually believe in levelling – but the name stuck. The Diggers (often referred to as the "true Levellers") were the group with this genuinely radical vision. They were part of the same seventeenth-century religious and political ferment that gave rise to Quakerism, and their leader, Gerrard Winstanley, was among London Quakers at certain times of his life.[19] 'Levelling' is the Quaker testimony to equality, given a political edge.

And *fourthly*, we need to act – for our own sakes as well as for the greater good: activism is good for us. Even a very small engagement can boost our sense of vitality and well-being.[20]

You may know the 1969 film musical *Goodbye Mr Chips*, or may have heard its signature song:

> In the morning of my life I shall look to the sunrise,
> At a moment in my life when the world is new.
> And the blessing I shall ask is that God will grant me,
> To be brave and strong and true,
> And to fill the world with love my whole life through.
>
> In the noontime of my life I shall look to the sunshine,
> At a moment in my life when the sky is blue.
> And the blessing I shall ask shall remain unchanging,
> To be brave and strong and true,
> And to fill the world with love my whole life through.
>
> In the evening of my life I shall look to the sunset,
> At a moment in my life when the night is due.
> And the question I shall ask only I can answer.
> Was I brave and strong and true?
> Did I fill the world with love my whole life through?

When I was in Zimbabwe in the mid 1980s, this song was being used in morning assembly in the school where I was teaching, as if it were a hymn. It asks important questions, and has been recorded many times since, including by the Mormon Tabernacle Choir.

Being brave is not the same thing as not being afraid. Being brave is being afraid and doing the right thing anyway. The work appropriate to different life stages is embedded in the song; doing the right thing will involve different actions at different points in our lives.

To my own cohort – often tagged as the post-war baby boom generation – I want to say this: by accident of birth our generation has, in many ways, been given the best of what the modern world had to offer, and subsequent generations will not have those benefits. We had the post-war settlement of universal free education, the welfare state and the NHS; we had antibiotics without resistant strains of bacteria; we had the pill without AIDS; in Britain, our generation has not had to fight a war; we had rising economic prosperity; we grew up believing we could change the world. As we stand at perhaps the summit of our working lives, we stand simultaneously at the summit of industrialised society as we have known it. We benefited hugely from the massive industrial expansion that characterised the second half of the twentieth century – and as we approach retirement we are beginning to know what that has cost the planet. Even if we escape the worst effects ourselves (and it's a big 'if'), our children and our grandchildren will not.

"From those to whom much is given, much is expected" (Luke 12:48). We have been given much, so what are we going to do with our active retirement years? There are a lot of us; we changed the face of politics when we were young – we could do so again. I believe that we owe a debt of gratitude, and have a responsibility to do what we can as individuals and collectively.

To young people, just embarking on the steps into adult life, I want to say this: as you look at the options ahead of you in terms of education, life skills and future work, consider what will be the truly essential skills in the future, the "really useful knowledge"[21] that you will need in the changed world that is coming. If you plan to go to university, either study something practical (engineering, medicine, agriculture, etc.) or – if you want to study for pleasure, enrichment and interest – start preparing now to acquire additional skills which will be the ones you will need to support yourself and contribute to the life of your community, whatever that is. Everyone needs to learn how to grow food, how to make, mend and fix things. Between us, as extended families, networks of friends and local communities, we need to take back all the hand-skills that the modern world has outsourced to mass production. Also, take care to develop your soft skills – facilitation, leadership, conflict-handling, and learning how to build community around you, wherever you are in your life.

To older people, perhaps feeling that you have moved beyond an exterior active life: remember that you have skills and knowledge that need to be passed on to subsequent generations; consider how you may be able to ensure that your knowledge, skills and experience do not die with you.

And to everyone else – the large adult group that sits between these bookend life stages – start now to acquire these new skills and attitudes for yourselves, and help to ensure that your children and grandchildren realise how essential and significant they are. This applies equally, of course, to those of us who do not have our own biological children and grandchildren. Just as we are all crew, we are all the parents and grandparents of humanity's next generations.

The Pale Blue Dot (NASA/JPL, 1990)

'The **Pale Blue Dot**' is a photograph of planet Earth. It was taken in 1990 by the spacecraft *Voyager 1*. At the request of Carl Sagan, NASA commanded the spacecraft, having completed its primary mission and now leaving the Solar System, to turn its camera around and to take a photograph of Earth across a great expanse of space – roughly four billion miles.

Carl Sagan said of this image:

Look again at that dot. That's here, that's home, that's us. On it every-one you love, everyone you know, everyone you ever heard of, every human being who ever was, lived out their lives. The aggregate of our joy and suffering, thousands of confident religions, ideologies, and economic doctrines, every hunter and forager, every hero and coward, every creator and destroyer of civilization, every king and peasant, every young couple in love, every mother and father, hopeful child, inventor and explorer, every teacher of morals, every corrupt politi-cian, every "superstar", every "supreme leader", every saint and sinner in the history of our species lived there – on a mote of dust suspended in a sunbeam.

Our posturings, our imagined self-importance, the delusion that we have some privileged position in the Universe, are challenged by this point of pale light. Our planet is a lonely speck in the great enveloping cosmic dark. In our obscurity, in all this vastness, there is no hint that help will come from elsewhere to save us from ourselves.

The Earth is the only world known so far to harbor life. There is nowhere else, at least in the near future, to which our species could mi-grate. Visit, yes. Settle, not yet. Like it or not, for the moment the Earth is where we make our stand. There is perhaps no better demonstration of the folly of human conceits than this distant image of our tiny world. To me, it underscores our responsibility to deal more kindly with one another, and to preserve and cherish the pale blue dot, the only home we've ever known.[22]

This is it; this is home – this is Earth and it's the only one we have. One-planet living isn't just a nice campaigning slogan. We either achieve one-planet living or we all perish.

We only get one trip to Earth, we only get one life. We get, you might say, the trip of a lifetime. And at the end of our life, when we look back, will we see that we have only been tourists? Will we realise that we saw the sights and looked at the scenery, we stared at the natives and used what we wanted for our pleasure, leaving the place poorer and more polluted than when we arrived? Or will we look back and know that we belonged here, we became part of the community, we contributed to the common good, we made a difference?

This is not only about the choices that each individual 'I' must make. It is about us as the gathered body of Quakers, as the Religious Society of Friends, in Britain and around the world. It is about us as a people of God, as a people of faith, alongside all other peoples of faith. It is about us as the human community, all of us together, all of us part of the community of all living beings on Earth.

In the evening of our lives we shall look to the sunset,
At a moment in our lives when the night is due.
And the question we shall ask only we can answer.
Were we brave? – we are going to need to be brave;
Were we strong? – we will need to be strong, we will need to be very strong, for and with each other;
Were we true? – we are going to need every bit of what our tradition bequeaths to us about truth in all its forms.

And now I'm going to modify the last line, but it will still scan, so it can still be sung:

Did we treat the Earth with love our whole life through?

In his sermon at Copenhagen Cathedral at the time of the 2009 climate summit, Rowan Williams, the Archbishop of Canterbury, said:

Love casts out fear. If we begin from the belief that God wants us to rejoice and delight in the created world, our basic attitude to the environment will not be anxiety or the desperate search for ways of controlling it; it will be the excited and hopeful search for understanding it and honouring its goodness and its complex, interdependent beauty.[23]

And in the final chapter of his book *Our choice: A plan to solve the climate crisis*, Al Gore describes two scenarios – we act, now, effectively; or we fail. He imagines a future generation, not that far ahead, looking back and asking either "What were you thinking? Didn't you hear the warnings from the scientists? Didn't you care?" or "How did you find the moral courage to rise up and solve a crisis so many said was impossible to solve?"

Gore produces an answer, of sorts, to the first question – "almost too painful to write," he says. He also answers the second question, setting out the path we could have followed to that future point. Written before the 2009 Copenhagen climate summit, he accurately anticipates its outcome as "timid", but then describes our subsequent actions, not without their problems and dangers, but resourceful and effective. In his final paragraph, apparently addressing this imagined future generation but in reality, of course, speaking now to us, his readers, he writes:

The choice is awesome and potentially eternal. It is in the hands of the present generation: a decision we cannot escape, and a choice to be mourned or celebrated through all the generations that follow.[24]

Dear Friends, let us take heed.

GLOSSARY

10:10 campaign
10:10 is a project that aimed initially to unite every sector of British society behind the idea that, by working together, we could achieve a 10 per cent cut in the UK's carbon emissions during 2010. See: http://www.1010uk.org

Carbon dioxide equivalent
There are various **greenhouse gases** that contribute to **climate change**, and most biological or chemical processes emit a mixture of them. Different gases have different warming potential and persist for different lengths of time in the atmosphere. To make comparisons possible, both of these properties are converted into carbon dioxide equivalence.

Carbon emissions
Carbon dioxide and carbon monoxide, produced by the burning of **fossil fuels** in industrial processes, electricity generation, domestic heating, motor transport, etc. These gases accumulate in the atmosphere, causing **global warming**.

Carbon footprint
A measure of the impact our activities have on the environment, and in particular on **climate change**. It relates to the amount of **greenhouse gases** produced in our day-to-day lives, through burning **fossil fuels** for electricity, heating and transportation, etc. The carbon footprint quantifies all the greenhouse gases we individually produce, directly or indirectly, and is measured in tonnes (or kg) of "**carbon dioxide equivalent**".

Climate change
A change in the statistical distribution of weather over periods of time that range from decades to millions of years. It can be a change in the average weather or in the distribution of weather events around an average (for example, greater or fewer extreme weather events). Climate change may be limited to a specific region, or may

occur across the whole Earth. In recent usage, climate change usually refers to changes in our modern climate (since the Industrial Revolution of the eighteenth century). It is sometimes referred to as anthropogenic climate change (i.e. caused by human activity); more generally known as **global warming**.

Concern
A Quaker term denoting an issue or action that an individual Friend or group of Friends feels led by the Spirit to take up as matter for some kind of ongoing action. The action could for instance involve prayer, fundraising, campaigning, voluntary practical involvement, awareness-raising, direct action, offers of service, and so on.

Contraction and convergence
A proposed global framework for reducing **greenhouse gas** emissions to combat **climate change**. It consists of reducing overall emissions of greenhouse gases to a safe level (contraction), and bringing everyone to a per capita level which is equal for all countries (convergence).

Copenhagen climate summit
Held 7–18 December 2009, the 15th Conference of the Parties to the **UN Framework Convention on Climate Change** (UNFCCC) met to negotiate agreements for countries to reduce **greenhouse gas** emissions, as their current commitments under the **Kyoto Protocol** expire in 2012. Two years earlier, at a previous UN climate conference in Bali, all UN governments had agreed on a timetable that would ensure a strong climate deal by the time of the Copenhagen conference. This was not achieved.

Deep ecology
A contemporary ecological philosophy that recognises the inherent worth of all other beings, regardless of their utility to humanity. The philosophy emphasises the interdependent nature of human and non-human life as well as the importance of ecosystems and natural processes. It provides a foundation for the environmental, ecological and green movements and has fostered a new set of environmental

ethics. The phrase "deep ecology" was coined by the Norwegian philosopher Arne Næss in 1973.

Deforestation

The permanent destruction of indigenous forests and woodlands. The term does not include the removal of industrial forests such as plantations of gums or pines. Deforestation has resulted in the reduction of indigenous forests to four-fifths of their pre-agricultural area. Indigenous forests now cover 21 per cent of the Earth's land surface.

DEFRA

The UK government department responsible for policy and regulations on the environment, food and rural affairs.

Earth Overshoot Day

A measure of human demand on the Earth's natural systems is known as our environmental footprint. It compares human demand with the planet's capacity to regenerate itself. It represents the area of biologically productive land and sea needed: a) to regenerate the resources that the humanity consumes; and b) to absorb and render harmless the corresponding waste. This measure makes it possible to estimate how many planet Earths it would take to support humanity if everybody lived a given lifestyle. For 2009 (the most recent year for which figures are available, at time of writing), humanity's total ecological footprint was very nearly 1.5 planets (up from 1.4 in 2006). This is an average, within which we find, for instance, 2.5 planets for the average European, 3.4 for Britain, 5 planets for the USA, and 0.4 for India. Within each country or region there are wide individual and regional variations. Another way of looking at this is to calculate the date each year when humanity, globally, goes into ecological deficit – when that year's 'environmental budget' has been spent. This is known as Earth Overshoot Day, a concept created by the New Economics Foundation. In 2009 it was 25 September. In 2010 it was 21 August. The date for 2011 was not available at the time this book went to press. See http://www.footprintnetwork.org

Eco-justice

This and similar terms are used in a variety of ways, but core to all of them is the idea that the pains and gains of environmental change, degradation, regeneration, etc. should be shared equally between all people. It is most often used to indicate that poor people (whether in the domestic or global context) should not bear a disproportionate weight of the negative effects of **climate change**, which is largely produced by richer people.

Energy descent

The continual decline in net energy available to support humanity. This decline is a mirror-image of the huge increase in energy use that has taken place during and since the Industrial Revolution. It also refers to a future scenario in which humanity has successfully adapted to the lower available energy, becoming more localised and self-reliant. It is a term favoured by people viewing peak energy as an opportunity for positive change, rather than an inevitable disaster.

Food insecurity

The opposite of food security, defined as the availability of food *and* access to it. A household is considered food secure when its occupants do not live in hunger or fear of starvation. Worldwide, roughly 852 million people are chronically hungry due to extreme poverty, while up to 2 billion people lack food security intermittently due to varying degrees of poverty or political/military conflict. Six million children die of hunger every year.

Fossil fuel

A hydrocarbon deposit (i.e. one made up of carbon and hydrogen), such as petroleum, coal or natural gas, derived from living matter (plant or animal) of a previous geologic era and now used for fuel.

Generational justice

At a minimum, this implies conserving enough of the natural environment to ensure that future generations will have the same opportunities in life as current generations. The idea of not mortgaging the life of subsequent generations to pay for our present way of living has both economic and environmental implications.

Global warming

The increase in the average temperature of the Earth's atmosphere, air and oceans since the mid-twentieth century, and its projected continuation. The Intergovernmental Panel on Climate Change (IPCC) has concluded that most of the observed temperature increase since the middle of the twentieth century was caused by increasing concentrations of **greenhouse gases** resulting from human activity such as the burning of **fossil fuels** (exacerbated by **deforestation**).

Greenhouse gases

Gases in a planet's atmosphere that absorb and emit solar radiation. The primary greenhouse gases in the Earth's atmosphere are water vapour, carbon dioxide, methane, nitrous oxide and ozone. Greenhouse gases greatly affect the temperature of the Earth; without them, the Earth's surface would be on average about 33°C (59°F) colder than at present. Since the beginning of the Industrial Revolution, the burning of fossil fuels has substantially increased the levels of carbon dioxide in the atmosphere.

Intentional community

A planned residential community, designed to have a much higher degree of cooperation and shared work than other communities. The members of an intentional community typically hold a common social, political, religious and/or spiritual vision. They will also usually share responsibilities and resources. Intentional communities include cohousing, ecovillages, communes and some housing cooperatives. New members are chosen by the community's existing membership.

The Kyoto Protocol

An international agreement linked to the **United Nations Framework Convention on Climate Change**. The major feature of the Kyoto Protocol is that it sets binding targets for 37 industrialised countries and the European community for reducing greenhouse gas emissions. These reductions amount to an average of five per cent, against 1990 levels, over the five-year period 2008–2012. The major distinction between the Protocol and the Convention is that while the Convention *encouraged* industrialised countries to stabilize greenhouse gas emissions, the Protocol *commits* them to do so.

Low carbon communities

Groups of people (typically a street, neighbourhood, village, etc.) working together to manage energy more efficiently, and consequently to reduce their bills. Some will be using cutting-edge technology to create their own energy, connecting homes, local businesses and public buildings to renewable sources. Some will focus more on insulation and reducing their demand for energy. Low carbon communities use fewer car miles, walk and cycle more and support good public transport. These communities support locally grown food. See: http://lowcarboncommunities.net

One-planet living

The concept of one-planet living uses ten principles of sustainability as a framework to help us enjoy a high quality of life, whilst using only our fair share of the Earth's resources. The ten principles are: zero carbon; zero waste; sustainable transport; sustainable materials; local and sustainable food; sustainable water; natural habitats and wildlife; cultural heritage; equity, fair trade and local economy; health and happiness. See: http://www.oneplanetliving.org

Peak oil

The point in time when the maximum rate of global petroleum extraction is reached, after which the rate of production enters irreversible decline. The concept is based on the observed production rates of individual oil wells and the combined production rate of a field of related oil wells. The accumulated production rate from an oil field over time usually grows exponentially until the rate peaks. It then declines, sometimes rapidly, until the field is depleted. Peak oil is often confused with oil depletion; peak oil is the point of maximum production rate while depletion refers to a period of falling reserves and supply.

Responsibility to Protect (R2P)

A norm or set of principles based on the idea that sovereignty is not a privilege, but a responsibility. R2P currently focuses on preventing and halting four crimes: genocide, war crimes, crimes against humanity and ethnic cleansing. In the international community R2P is a norm, not a law. R2P provides a framework for using tools that already exist (such as mediation, confidence building measures, early warning mechanisms and economic sanctions) to prevent mass atrocities. Civil society organisations, nation states, regional organisations and international institutions all have a part to play in making R2P a functioning reality.

Restorative justice

An approach to justice that focuses on the needs of victims and offenders rather than on the need to satisfy abstract principles of law, or on the community's need to exact punishment. Victims are given an active role in the resolution of a dispute, and offenders are encouraged to take responsibility for their actions and to repair the harm they have caused.

Transition

A Transition Initiative is a community working together to look at **peak oil** and **climate change** and address this question: "For all those aspects of life that this community needs in order to sustain itself and thrive, how do we significantly increase resilience (to mitigate the effects of peak oil) and drastically reduce carbon emissions (to mitigate the effects of climate change)?" See: http://www.transitiontowns.org

UN Framework Convention on Climate Change

UNFCCC was adopted on 9 May 1992, and signed by more than 190 countries at the Earth Summit in Rio de Janeiro. The Convention contains general principles to stabilise **greenhouse gases** at a level in the atmosphere that would prevent dangerous human-induced **climate change**.

Water footprint
An indicator that looks at both direct and indirect water use of a consumer or producer. The water footprint is defined as the total volume of fresh water that is used to produce the goods and services consumed by an individual or community, or produced by a business. See: http://www.waterfootprint.org

Woodbrooke Quaker Study Centre
A residential adult study and retreat centre, set on the south side of the city of Birmingham in the English Midlands. It runs a year-round programme of short courses and conferences and offers off-site teaching programmes for Quaker meetings. Additionally, it produces occasional study packs and online learning materials and hosts meetings and conferences on a commercial basis. The Swarthmore Lecture is overseen by Woodbrooke Trustees. See: http://www.woodbrooke.org.uk

Some of the entities in this glossary have been adapted from http://www.wikipedia.org. Further information on all of these terms, and others, may be found:

- on http://www.wikipedia.org
- at http://www.climatefruitandwine.co.za/download/SOW09_Climate%20Guide-Glossary.pdf (final five pages)
- or in Bob Henson, *The Rough Guide to Climate Change* (*Rough Guides Reference Titles*) (London: Rough Guides Ltd, 2006).

NOTES

Introduction

1. See: James Howard Kunstler, *The long emergency: Surviving the converging catastrophes of the twenty-first century* (London: Atlantic Books, 2005); the author explores the same themes in fictional form in *World made by hand* (New York: Atlantic Monthly Press, 2008) and *The witch of Hebron* (New York: Atlantic Monthly Press, 2010).
2. http://www.transitionnetwork.org/support/what-transition-initiative
3. Harry Patch (with Richard van Emden), *The last fighting Tommy: The life of Harry Patch, the only surviving veteran of the trenches* (London: Bloomsbury, 2007), p. 71.

Chapter 1 – Only one Earth

1. Carl Sagan, *Cosmos* (London: Macdonald Futura Publishers, 1980), p. 345.
2. C. G. Jung, *Memories, dreams, reflections* (London: Fontana, 1967), p. 320.
3. Published in the UK as: Donella H. Meadows *et al*, *The limits to growth: A report for the Club of Rome's Project on the Predicament of Mankind* (London: Pan), 1974.
4. Quoted in Robert Poole, *Earthrise: How man first saw the Earth* (London: Yale University Press, 2008), p. 160.
5. James Lovelock, *Gaia: A new look at life on earth* (Oxford University Press, 1979).
6. Peter Bakken *et al*, *Ecology, justice, and Christian faith: A critical guide to the literature* (Santa Barbara (CA): Greenwood Press, 1995), pp. 11–12.
7. Matthew Fox, *Original blessing: A primer in creation spirituality presented in four paths, twenty-six themes, and two questions* (Santa Fe (NM): Bear & Co, 1983).
8. Quoted in Poole, *Earthrise*, p. 104.
9. *In the shadow of the moon*, DVD (UK edition 2007).
10. http://www.nasa.gov/mission_pages/constellation/main/A13_panel.html

11. See: Alice Roberts, *The incredible human journey* (London: Bloomsbury, 2009); Robin Dunbar, *The human story* (London: Faber and Faber, 2005).

12. Of course, further back than humanity, we are kin to all life on Earth, through the process of evolution. For instance, we share about one third of our genes with daffodils; the chemical formulae for haemoglobin (that carries oxygen in our blood) and chlorophyll (that enables plants to photosynthesise) are identical except for one atom – iron in haemoglobin, magnesium in chlorophyll (the formulae are, respectively, $C_{55}H_{72}FeN_4O_6$ and $C_{55}H_{72}MgN_4O_6$). For an account of humanity's place in the evolutionary process, see: Richard Dawkins, *The greatest show on earth: The evidence for evolution* (London: Black Swan, 2010).

13. For more detail, see Martin Rees, *Before the beginning: Our universe and others* (London: Perseus Books, 1998), ch. 1.

14. Chris Cleave, 'Down with the Kids', *The Guardian 'Family'*, 2 May 2009. http://www.guardian.co.uk/lifeandstyle/2009/may/02/down-with-kids-chris-cleave

15. It looks likely that the 2011 date will be a little later than in 2010, as the effects of the global economic turn-down take effect (personal communication from Nicole Freeling, of Global Footprint Network, June 2011).

16. Margaret Atwood, *Payback: Debt and the shadow side of wealth* (London: Bloomsbury, 2008), ch. 5.

Chapter 2 – What kind of community?

1. Rachel Carson, *Silent spring* (Boston (MA): Houghton Mifflin, 1962).

2. Rainer Maria Rilke (M.D. Herter Norton, trans.), *Letters to a young poet* (London: Norton, revised ed. 1954 [1934]), Letter Four (16 July 1903), p. 35.

3. Though it is, of course, not that simple: among the Amish, behaviour contrary to community norms can lead to being 'shunned'. Acceptance and belonging are not unconditional.

4. *The Rule of St. Benedict* (Mineola (NY): Dover Publications, 2007), p. 56.

5. *Quaker faith & practice: The book of Christian discipline of the*

Yearly Meeting of the Religious Society of Friends (Quakers) in Britain (London: The Yearly Meeting of the Religious Society of Friends (Quakers) in Britain, 1995).

6. Originally published in Parker J Palmer, *A place called community* (Pendle Hill Pamphlet 212) (Wallingford (PA): Pendle Hill Publications, 1977), p. 15.

7. See, for instance, Pink Dandelion, *An introduction to Quakerism* (Cambridge: Cambridge University Press, 2007), ch. 3.

8. *Opening the door: The Spiritual Hospitality Project report* (Lampeter: Meeting of Friends in Wales, 2003), p. 50.

9. Harvey Gillman, *Spiritual hospitality: A Quaker's understanding of outreach* (Pendle Hill Pamphlet 314) (Wallingford (PA): Pendle Hill Publications, 2003), p. 13.

10. Personal communication from Susan Robson, May 2011; publication forthcoming.

11. Roger Sawtell, 'Not the Damascus Road', *Journal of Woodbrooke College*, Issue No. 2, Winter 1992/93, pp. 12–19.

12. Sawtell, 'Not the Damascus Road', p. 19.

13. http://www.cohousing.org.uk

14. http://today.yougov.co.uk/life/no-longer-such-good-neighbours

15. http://transitionculture.org

16. http://transitionculture.org/2006/09/04/why-the-survivalists-have-got-it-wrong

17. http://www.incredible-edible-todmorden.co.uk. This was the first, and other 'Incredible Edibles' have since sprung up.

18. Paul Clarke, speaking at a Good Lives weekend at Woodbrooke, 26 June 2010.

19. As sea levels rise, the British Isles will experience some coastal flooding, and increased rainfall in particular areas is likely to increase local flooding. However, Britain is not expected, under current estimates, to suffer widespread catastrophic flooding.

20. James Lovelock, *The vanishing face of Gaia: A final warning* (London: Allen Lane, 2009), pp. 11–13.

21. A storm large enough to produce a significant coronal mass ejection could produce substantial global damage. Such an event in 1859 burned out the world's entire telegraph network. In 1989 a solar storm less intense than that of 1859 disabled the power grid

over the whole of Quebec. In 1994 such an event disabled communications satellites, again over Canada. Peaks of solar storms occur roughly on an 11-year cycle.

22. See also: Susan Maushart, *The winter of our disconnect: How one family pulled the plug on their technology and lived to tell/text/tweet the tale* (London: Profile Books, 2011).

23. See, for instance, Christina Baldwin and Anne Linnea, *The circle way: A leader in every chair* (San Francisco: Berrett-Koehler, 2010); Christina Baldwin, *Calling the circle: The first and future culture* (New York: Bantam Books, 1998); Margaret Wheatley, *Turning to one another: Simple conversations to restore hope to the future* (San Francisco: Berrett-Koehler, 2009).

24. From Marianne Williamson, *A return to love: Reflections on the principles of 'A course in miracles'* (New York: HarperCollins, 1992), p. 191.

Chapter 3 – What does a good life look like?

1. NIV
2. http://www.un.org/millenniumgoals
3. http://www.micahchallenge.org.uk/
4. http://www.independent.co.uk/news/world/americas/the-good-life-in-havana-cubas-green-revolution-410930.html. See also DVD referred to on p. 122.
5. http://thegoodlife.wwf.ca/Home.cfm
6. Attributed to the Pachamama Alliance (http://www.pachamama.org). The exact figures are disputed, but the point is nevertheless well made.
7. See for instance a recent report: Felicity Lawrence, 'How Peru's wells are being sucked dry by British love of asparagus', *The Guardian*, 15 September 2010. http://www.guardian.co.uk/environment/2010/sep/15/peru-asparagus-british-wells
8. http://www.waterfootprint.org
9. http://www.fera.defra.gov.uk/aboutUs/documents/launch/bob-Watson.pdf
10. Alex Renton, 'Matters of taste', *Prospect*, January 2010, p. 16.
11. Wendell Berry, *The gift of good land: Further essays cultural and agricultural* (New York: North Point Press, 1982), p. 281.

12. http://www.celdf.org/Default.aspx?tabid=548
13. Begonia Filgueira and Ian Mason, 'Wild side of the law', *The Guardian*, 4 May 2009. http://www.guardian.co.uk/commentis-free/2009/may/04/climate-change-law
14. http://www.unep.org/Law/PDF/UNEPEnv-LawGuide&Princ N05.pdf
15. See, for instance, Robert Boyd, *Quaker ways in foreign policy* (London: Oxford University Press, 1960), especially chapters 11 and 12.
16. Now Quaker Concern for Animals: http://www.all-creatures. org/qa/aboutus.html
17. Paul Lacey, *The unequal world we inhabit: Quaker responses to terrorism and fundamentalism* (Swarthmore Lecture 2010) (London: Quaker Books, 2010), pp. 78–84. See also: James Pattison, *Humanitarian intervention and the responsibility to protect: Who should intervene?* (Oxford: Oxford University Press, 2010).
18. James Barber, of Imperial College, London, estimates that each year humanity burns the quantity of fossil fuels that took one million years to accumulate. http://www.en.globaltalentnews. com/current_news/news/120/Artificial-photosynthesis-as-an-alternative-to-fossil-fuels.html
19. Jeremy Rifkin, speaking at the RSA, London, 15 March 2010. See also Jeremy Rifkin, *The empathic civilisation: The race to global consciousness in a world in crisis* (London: Polity, 2010).
20. Fox, George, (J. L. Nickalls, ed.). *The journal of George Fox* (Cambridge: University Press, 1952), p. 263.
21. Richard Wilkinson and Kate Pickett, *The spirit level: Why equality is better for everyone* (London: Penguin, 2009).
22. http://www.equalitytrust.org.uk/why/evidence
23. See, for instance, for the whole section over the next four pages of this chapter: Dan Ariely, *Predictably irrational: The hidden forces that shape our decisions* (New York: Harper Perennial, 2010); David Boyle and Andrew Simms, *The New Economics: A bigger picture* (London: Earthscan, 2009); Nicholas Christakis and James Fowler, *Connected: The surprising power of our social networks and how they shape our lives* (New York: Little Brown, 2009); Frans de Waal, *The age of empathy: Nature's lessons for*

a kinder society (London, Souvenir Press, 2009); Robin Dunbar, *How many friends does one person need? Dunbar's number and other evolutionary quirks* (London: Faber and Faber, 2010); Michael Gazzaniga, *Human: The science behind what makes us unique* (New York: HarperCollins, 2008); Rick Hanson and Richard Mendius, *Buddha's brain: The practical neuroscience of happiness, love, and wisdom* (Oakland (CA): New Harbinger Publications, 2009); Jonah Lehrer, *How we decide* (New York: Houghton Mifflin Harcourt, 2009); Michael Tomasello, *Why we cooperate* (London: The MIT Press, 2009).

24. Discussed in Ariely, *Predictably irrational*, p. 250.
25. Dieter Birnbacher, 'What motivates us to care for the (distant) future?' in Alex Gosseries and Lukas Meyer, eds, *Intergenerational justice* (Oxford: Oxford University Press, 2009), pp. 273–300.
26. Fox, George, (J. L. Nickalls, ed.). *The journal of George Fox* (*Cambridge: University Press, 1952*), p. 263.

Chapter 4 – How long is "sustainable"?

1. http://www.brianswimme.org/media/excerpts.asp
2. http://www.beyondintractability.org/audio/elise_boulding/?nid=2413
3. Ed van Hinte *et al, Smart architecture* (Rotterdam: 010 Publishers, 2003).
4. Jean Giono, trans Barbara Bray, *The man who planted trees* (London: Harvill, 1995).
5. http://en.wikisource.org/wiki/Giono_letter_to_Digne_official
6. Jan Zalasiewicz, *The earth after us: What legacy will humans leave in the rocks?* (Oxford: Oxford University Press, 2009), p. 2.
7. Carl Sagan, *The dragons of Eden: Speculations on the evolution of human intelligence* (London: Hodder & Stoughton, 1977), ch. 1.
8. Sagan, *The dragons of Eden*, p. 17. We have to forgive him for '*man*kind' – this was 1977!
9. For a time-chart that projects into the future as long as we have looked at the past, see http://www.historyoftheuniverse.com/tl1.html
10. Narrator speaking on 'Wheeling and dealing', part 2 of *The day the world took off*, first broadcast on Channel 4 in 2000; now

available at http://www.youtube.com/watch?v=81xBNudz7O8

11. Stewart Brand, *The clock of the long now: Time and responsibility* (London: Phoenix, 2000).

12. The phrase "deep time" originated with the eighteenth-century Scottish geologist, James Hutton, to refer to geologic time. It is also used in Joanna Macy's deep ecology work, to visualise contact between ancestors and descendants of those involved in the exercise.

13. http://www.longnow.org

14. http://www.longnow.org/about

15. http://www.makingthemodernworld.org.uk/icons_of_invention/technology/1968-2000/IC.106/

16. John Seed *et al*, *Thinking like a mountain: Towards a council of all beings* (Philadelphia: New Society Publishers, 1988), p. 36.

17. Nick Lane, 'The cradle of life', *New Scientist*, 17 October 2009, pp. 38–42.

18. But in thinking about how much time we have to act, remember that 02010 already brought us devastating drought and forest fires in Russia, overwhelming flooding in Pakistan; and in Australia, bushfires, drought, and then severe flooding at the end of the year.

19. Pink Dandelion, *The liturgies of Quakerism* (Aldershot: Ashgate, 2005), p. 41.

20. The cartoon is not, alas, reproduced here, as we have no provenance or copyright permission for it.

21. This quotation, in different variations, is variously attributed to Charles Dickens (for which I can find no evidence), Norfolk famers, New England (USA), old proverb and general farming tradition.

Chapter 5 – We are all crew

1. John Wilhelm Rowntree, quoted by H.G. Wood, in Ralph Barlow (David Gray, ed.), *Woodbrooke 1953-1978: A documentary account of Woodbrooke's third 25 years* (York: Sessions, 1982), p. 6.

2. First published research: B. Latane and J. Darley, 'Bystander "Apathy"', *American Scientist*, 1969, 57, 244–268.

3. This incident has more recently been explored in fictional form:

Ryan David Jahn, *Acts of violence* (London: Macmillan, 2009). An economist and a journalist, co-authors, claim to have uncovered errors in the original press reporting of the incident. Their comments, however, have no bearing on the body of subsequent research. See Steven Levitt and Stephen Dubner, *Superfreakonomics* (London: Penguin, 2009), ch. 3.

4. http://www.uwlax.edu/faculty/cerbin/ls/PSY%20Research%20 Lesson%20Model%20of%20Bystander%20Intervention.htm

5. James Howard Kunstler, *The long emergency: Surviving the converging catastrophes of the twenty-first century* (London: Atlantic, 2005).

6. Dan Gardner, *Risk: The science and politics of fear* (London: Virgin Books, 2008).

7. Al Gore, *An inconvenient truth*, DVD, 2008.

8. Franny Armstrong, *The age of stupid*, DVD, 2009.

9. http://www.ecoamerica.net/sites/default/files/press/ecoAm_ Climate_Energy_Truths.pdf

10. Quoted with permission from Viewpoint Learning, Inc., *Listening to the public: Understanding and overcoming barriers to sustainability, Executive Summary* (San Diego, CA: Viewpoint Learning, 2006).

11. I am indebted to Marion McNaughton for drawing my attention to this.

12. Eva Fogelman, *Conscience and courage: Rescuers of Jews during the Holocaust* (London: Cassell, 1995).

13. "The universe exists on the merit of the righteous among the nations of the world, and they are privileged to see the Divine Presence", *Babylonian Talmud*.

14. Iris Murdoch, *The sovereignty of good* (London: Routledge, 2000 [1970]), p. 36.

15. Giles Fraser, 'Greater love hath no man', BBC Radio 4, 3 April 2010. http://www.bbc.co.uk/programmes/b00rmxk9

16. James Hansen, *Storms of my grandchildren: The truth about the coming climate catastrophe and our last chance to save humanity* (London: Bloomsbury, 2009), pp. 184, 277.

17. Gustavo Esteva, 'The arrogance of Cancún', *The Guardian*, 16 December 2010. http://www.guardian.co.uk/commentisfree/cif-

green/2010/dec/15/cancun-governments-play-god

18. See: Quaker Peace and Service, *Deeds, not creeds: Insights on Friends' peace testimony at Yearly Meeting 1993* (London: Quaker Peace and Service, 1993).

19. This idea was suggested to me independently by both Peter Reid and Simon Beard.

Chapter 6 – The time is now

1. Karl Marx, *Theses on Feuerbach* (thesis 11) in Lawrence Simon (ed), *Selected writings of Karl Marx* (Indianapolis (IN): Hackett, 1994), p. 98.

2. Marcello Musto (ed.), *Karl Marx's Grundrisse: Foundations of the critique of political economy 150 years later* (London: Routledge, 2008) p. 101.

3. T. S. Eliot, 'Little Gidding', *Four Quartets* (London: Faber, 2001).

4. The high level of response to the 2010 *Friends Quarterly* essay competition shows that many Friends are engaged with this question – see http://www.thefriend.co.uk/fq

5. Jan Zalasiewicz, *The Earth after us: What legacy will humans leave in the rocks?* (Oxford: OUP, 2008), p. 192.

6. James Lovelock, *Gaia: A new look at life on Earth* (Oxford: OUP, 1979).

7. See for instance: C. P. Michael and M. C. Norrisey, *Prayer and temperament: Different forms for different personality types* (Charlottesville (VA): The Open Door, 1984). Suzanne Zuercher, *Using the Enneagram in prayer: A contemplative guide* (Notre Dame (IN): Ave Maria Press, 2008). Suzanne Zuercher, *Enneagram spirituality: From compulsion to contemplation* (Notre Dame (IN): Ave Maria Press, 1992).

8. W. H. Murray, *The Scottish Himalayan expedition* (London: J. M. Dent and Sons, 1951), p. 6.

9. George Mcleod, founder of the Iona Community, speaking when he was a Church of Scotland Minister in Govan; see http://www.galgael.org/folk/ourpeople

10. *Huffington Post*, 10 September 2009, http://www.huffingtonpost.com/franny-armstrong/the-age-of-stupid-gives-a_b_281903.html

11. Richard Bach, *Illusions: The adventures of a reluctant messiah* (London: Pan Books, 1978), p. 121.
12. There are some wonderful writers who exhibit this quality (rather than just talk about it). For example: Elizabeth Marshall Thomas, *The hidden life of deer: Lessons from the natural world* (New York: HarperCollins, 2009); Annie Dillard, *Pilgrim at Tinker Creek* (Norwich: Canterbury Press, 2011 [1974]); Mary Rose O'Reilley, *The barn at the end of the world: The apprenticeship of a Quaker, Buddhist shepherd* (Minneapolis (MN): Milkweed Editions, 2001).
13. Esther Sternberg, *Healing spaces: The science of place and well-being* (London: Belknap Press, 2009).
14. Ancient woodland is a term used in the United Kingdom to refer specifically to woodland dating back to 1600 or before in England and Wales, or 1750 in Scotland. Before this, planting of new woodland was uncommon, so a wood present in 1600 was likely to have developed naturally. In the USA the term used is old-growth forest (also termed primary forest, ancient forest, virgin forest, primeval forest, frontier forest); this is a forest which, containing trees which have attained great age with associated structural features, exhibits unique ecological features.
15. http://web.fi.ibimet.cnr.it/MMV4/data/files/Takayama_516-520.pdf
16. See, for instance, Marc Bekoff, *The animal manifesto: Six reasons for expanding our compassion footprint* (Novato (CA): New World Library, 2010).
17. 'How to Build Community' (available as attractive posters, postcards, bookmarks, etc., along with other themes) from: http://syracuseculturalworkers.com/poster-how-build-community
18. David Boyle and Andrew Simms, *The new economics: A bigger picture* (London: Earthscan, 2009), p. 172.
19. David Boulton, *Gerrard Winstanley and the Republic of Heaven* (Dent: Dales Historical Monographs, 1999).
20. M. Klar and T. Kasser, 'Some benefits of being an activist: Measuring activism and its role in psychological well-being', *Political Psychology*, 30 (5), 755–777, 2009.
21. Nineteenth-century workers distinguished the knowledge they

had chosen and sought out from the knowledge they learned on their bosses' behalf; they called the former "really useful knowledge".

22. Carl Sagan, *Pale blue dot: A vision of the human future in space* (New York: Random House, 1994), pp. 6–7.
23. 'Act for the sake of love: Archbishop preaches in Copenhagen Cathedral', Sunday 13 December 2009, http://www.archbishopofcanterbury.org/articles.php/765/act-for-the-sake-of-love-archbishop-preaches-in-copenhagen-cathedral/
24. Al Gore, *Our choice: A plan to solve the climate crisis* (London: Bloomsbury, 2009), p. 404.

FURTHER RESOURCES

Additional to items listed in the notes to each chapter, see pp. 111–121.

Chapter I – Only one Earth

Books and other written material
Tim Flannery, *Here on Earth: A new beginning* (London: Penguin Books, 2011).

David Petersen del Mar, *Environmentalism* (Harlow: Pearson Education, 2006).

Rod Pyle, *Destination moon: The Apollo missions in the astronauts' own words* (London: Carlton Books, 2005).

Bernard Wood, *Human evolution: A very short introduction* (Oxford: Oxford University Press, 2005).

DVDs and other visual material
Alice Roberts, *The incredible human journey* (DVD, UK edition, 2009).

Carl Sagan, *Cosmos* (DVD, UK edition, 2009 [1980]).

Web resources
NASA: http://www.nasa.gov

For lots of information, resources and activities: http://www.rainforestinfo.org.au/deep-eco/welcome.htm

Rowan Williams, 'The climate crisis: Fashioning a Christian response' (lecture given by the Archbishop of Canterbury, 13 October 2009, Southwark Cathedral, sponsored by Operation Noah). http://www.archbishopofcanterbury.org/articles.php/765/act-for-the-sake-of-love-archbishop-preaches-in-copenhagen-cathedral/

Chapter 2 – What kind of community?

Books and other written material

Jono Bacon, *The art of community: Building the new age of participation* (Farnham, UK: O'Reilly Media, 2009). See also: http://www.artofcommunityonline.org

Marek Kohn, *Turned out nice: How the British Isles will change as the world heats up* (London: Faber and Faber, 2010).

Alastair McIntosh, *Rekindling community: Connecting people, environment and spirituality* (Dartington: Green Books [for the Schumacher Society], 2008).

Thich Nhat Hanh and Jack Lawlor, *Friends on the path: Building and sustaining spiritual communities* (Berkeley (CA): Parallax Press, 2002).

DVDs and other visual material

The power of community: How Cuba survived peak oil (DVD). The story of the Cuban people's hardship after they lost access to Soviet oil in the early 1990s. In their own words, the people tell of their ingenuity and triumph over sudden adversity – through cooperation, conservation and community.
http://www.powerofcommunity.org

Chapter 3 – What does a good life look like?

Books and other written material

Thich Nhat Hanh, *The world we have: A Buddhist approach to peace and ecology* (Berkeley (CA): Parallax Press, 2008).

Leo Hickman (ed.), *A good life: The guide to ethical living* (revised edition) (London: Transworld Publishers, 2008).

Andrew Simms and Joe Smith, *Do good lives have to cost the earth?* (London: Constable, 2008).

Stella Thomas, *Hydropolitics: An introduction* (London: Zed Books, 2011).

DVDs and other visual material

In Transition (the first detailed film about the Transition movement, showing communities around the world responding to peak oil and climate change with creativity, imagination and humour, and setting about rebuilding their local economies and communities. It is positive, solutions-focused and fun).
Available at http://transitionculture.org/in-transition

To watch a video of Robert Watson's presentation [see p. 43], go to http://www.fera.defra.gov.uk/aboutUs/documents/launch/index.cfm?video=06

Web resources

Happy Planet Index: http://www.happyplanetindex.org

Chapter 4 – How long is sustainable?

Books and other written material

Shaun Chamberlain, *The Transition timeline: For a local, resilient future* (Dartington: Green Books, 2009).

Rob Hopkins, *The Transition handbook: From oil dependency to local resilience* (Dartington: Green Books, 2008).

Ann Morisy, *Borrowing from the future: A faith-based approach to intergenerational equity* (London: Continuum Books, 2011).

Pat Murphy, *Plan C: Community survival strategies for peak oil and climate change* (Philadelphia (PA): New Society Publishers, 2008).

Brian Swimme and Mary Evelyn Tucker, *Journey of the universe* (London: Yale University Press, 2011).
See also: http://www.journeyoftheuniverse.org/

DVDs and other visual material

SciAm [Scientific American], *The earth without humans*, 2007
http://www.youtube.com/watch?v=K5wP6m0d0xc

National Geographic, *When humans disappear*, 2008 http://www.youtube.com/watch?v=ri9bAtQDe00&feature=related

National Geographic, *Aftermath: Cities crumble*, 2008 http://www.youtube.com/watch?v=Rh-lqtxZisA&feature=channel

If you would like to work with a group to construct a timeline for the history of the Earth (rather than of the whole universe), there is an excellent method, needing a roll of toilet paper and a long corridor or large outdoor space. It is very informative and great fun, suitable for children's or all-age groups. Complete instructions may be found at: http://www.worsleyschool.net/science/files/toiletpaper/history.html

Chapter 5 – We are all crew

Books and other written material

Hope Babcock, 'Assuming personal responsibility for improving
the environment: Moving toward a new environmental norm',
Harvard Law Review, 2009/33, pp. 117–175. Available at: http://
www.law.harvard.edu/students/orgs/elr/vol33_1/Babcock.pdf

Pearl Oliner and Samuel Oliner, *The altruistic personality: Rescuers
of Jews in Nazi Europe* (New York: Free Press, 1988).

Sara Parkin, *The positive deviant: Sustainability leadership in a
perverse world* (London: Earthscan, 2010).

Adam Taylor, *Mobilizing hope: Faith-inspired activism for a post-civil
rights generation* (Downers Grove (IL): InterVarsity Press, 2010).

DVDs and other visual material

The first of a series on YouTube about bystander apathy – excellent
clip introducing and illustrating the issues:
http://www.youtube.com/watch?v=OSsPfbup0ac
On this page of YouTube you will also find links to other clips on
this theme.

Web resources

The 'Let's all take some personal responsibility for the environment
group' on Facebook:
http://www.facebook.com/group.php?gid=4931783146

Chapter 6 – The time is now

Books and other written material

Nafeez Mosaddeq Ahmed, *A user's guide to the crisis of civilization: And how to save it* (London: Pluto, 2010).

Karen Armstrong, *Twelve steps to a compassionate life* (London: Bodley Head, 2010).

Carolyn Baker, *Navigating the coming chaos: A handbook for inner transition* (Bloomington, IN: iUniverse, 2011).

Joanna Macy, *Coming back to life: Practices to reconnect our lives, our world* (Gabriola Island (BC): New Society Publishers, 1998).

Paul Murray, *The sustainable self: A personal approach to sustainability education* (London: Earthscan, 2011).

Arran Stibbe (ed.), *The handbook of sustainability literacy: Skills for a changing world* (Dartington: Green Books, 2009).

Web resources

Be the Change: http://bethechange.org.uk
Britain Yearly Meeting: http://www.quaker.org.uk
Community of Interbeing: http://www.ukspirituality.org
Living Witness Project: http://www.livingwitness.org.uk
Transition Network: http://www.transitionnetwork.org
UK Spirituality Network: http://www.ukspirituality.org
Woodbrooke Good Lives Project: http://www.woodbrooke.org.uk/goodlives

Works of fiction helping us to think in new ways about these issues

Steven Amsterdam
Things we didn't see coming (London: Harvill Secker, 2010)
Margaret Atwood
The handmaid's tale (London: Vintage Classics, 2010 [1986])
Oryx and Crake (London: Virago Press, 2004)
The year of the flood (London: Virago Press, 2010)
James Howard Kunstler
World made by hand (New York: Atlantic Monthly Press, 2008)
The witch of Hebron (New York: Atlantic Monthly Press, 2010)
Doris Lessing
The memoirs of a survivor (London: Flamingo, 1995 [1974])
Shikasta (London: Flamingo, 1994 [1979])
George Marshall
The Earth party: Love and revolution at a time of climate change (Brighton: Pen Press, 2009)
Kim Stanley Robinson, *Science in the capital* trilogy:
Forty signs of rain (London: HarperCollins, 2004)
Fifty degrees below (London: HarperCollins, 2006)
Sixty days and counting (London: HarperCollins, 2007)

Quaker material

Susannah Brindle and Alastair McIntosh, *Kinship with creation: Two Quakers share their views* (Quaker Green Action, 2002)

Joycelin Dawes, *Choosing life: Embracing spirituality in the 21st century* (Quaker Universalist Group Pamphlet 32, 2008)

Connie McPeak Green and Marty Paxson Grundy, *Matthew 18: Wisdom for living in community* (Pendle Hill Pamphlet 399) (Wallingford (PA): Pendle Hill Publications, 2008)

Jack Kirk, *Kindling a life of concern: Spirit-led Quaker action* (Pendle Hill Pamphlet 404) (Wallingford (PA): Pendle Hill Publications, 2009)

Alastair McIntosh, *Hell and high water: Climate change, hope and the human condition* (Edinburgh: Birlinn, 2008)

Rosemary Morrow, *A demanding and uncertain adventure: Exploration of a concern for Earth restoration and how we must live to pass on to our children – and their children, and all living things – an Earth restored* (James Bachhase Lecture 2011) (Glen Osmand: Religious Society of Friends (Quakers) in Australia, 2011)

Parker J. Palmer, *A place called community* (Pendle Hill Pamphlet 212) (Wallingford (PA): Pendle Hill Publications, 1977)

Quaker Green Action, *Walk cheerfully, step lightly* (Quaker Green Action, 2004)

Jennie Ratcliffe, *Integrity, ecology, and community* (Pendle Hill Pamphlet 403) (Wallingford (PA): Pendle Hill Publications, 2009).

Anne Thomas, *Only fellow voyagers: Creation stories as guides for the journey* (Swarthmore Lecture 1995) (London: Quaker Home Service, 1995).

See also:

http://www.livingwitness.org.uk/resources.htm [various resources]

http:// www.woodbrooke.org.uk/pages/downloads.html [study pack]

http:// www.quaker.org.uk/quaker-response-crisis-climate-change [Quaker statement on climate change]

http:// www.quaker.org.uk/responding-climate-change [briefing pack]

http:// www.alastairmcintosh.com [Alastair McIntosh's website]

STUDY/REFLECTION GUIDE

What follows is a study/reflection guide that can be used by groups or individuals. There is one session for each chapter of the book.

The appendices offer detailed guides to the suggested ways of working.

You are of course free to use the material in any way you wish.

If you are using this with a group, each session will work well in about 1½ hours with a group of about 8–12 people. If you have a much smaller group (perhaps 4 or 5 people) you will probably need about an hour. In each case, add extra at the start and end for shared worship, and for drinking tea together!

If you are using the guide by yourself, rather than in a group, then reflective writing (or journalling) is the suggested method.

In either case, you might want to have felt-tips or crayons available to make images, in addition to talking or writing.

Chapter 1 – Only one earth

Suggestions for reflection (in journalling or creative listening – see appendices – or any other way that works for you)

Choose one or two of these, as suits you (or the group you're working with); don't feel you have to plod through all three!

1. Take one or more of the biblical passages mentioned in this chapter (in any translation you like) and use in *lectio divina* (alone or in a group), creative listening/worship-sharing (see appendices), or Friendly Bible study.*

   a. The first chapter of Genesis
   b. Job 38:4–39, 12, and 42:1–6
   c. Psalm 24:1–6
   d. Psalm 104:1–30

2. Look at the Earth images reproduced on pages 8 and 13.
   a. If you remember the time before they existed: Can you recall how you felt when they appeared? In what ways are they still able to move you?
   b. If for you these images have always been there: What emotional or spiritual impact do they have for you? Does it make any difference to hear about their effect when they appeared?

3. One of the Apollo astronauts said: "I'm not a religious person . . . but I think, really, the whole Earth is the garden of Eden. We've been given a paradise to live in. I think about that every day."† If you 'thought about this every day', what might you be led to do differently in your life?

---

*Joanne and Larry Spears, *Friendly Bible study* (Philadelphia (PA): Friends General Conference, 1990).

†Quoted in Robert Poole, *Earthrise: How man first saw the Earth* (London: Yale University Press, 2008), p. 105.

Chapter 2 – What kind of community?

Suggestions for reflection (in journalling or creative listening – see appendices – or any other way that works for you)

These questions are designed to stimulate thinking about your own locality –not for responding to with straightforward answers.

1. **Mapping your community:** What kind of locality do you live in? What do you value about it? What does it lack (for you)? What do you need, or choose, to go outside your locality for?

2. **How does your local area function in practical terms as a community? How does it earn its living?** Where do people work? How locally, and with how much travelling? What proportion of ordinary needs can be met locally (e.g. shopping, food)? What essential practical needs are met from elsewhere? What cultural and spiritual needs are met locally, or elsewhere (in general, and for yourself personally)? What is, and isn't, within walking/cycling/bus-journey distance?

3. **What could be adapted for a more localised way of life?** For example: food, transport, your local Quaker meeting, social life, cultural life etc.

4. **Making a difference: Where can a difference be made?** Where can we start? What could you do personally? What could your Quaker meeting do?

Chapter 3 – What does a good life look like?

Suggestions for reflection (in journalling or creative listening – see appendices – or any other way that works for you)

1. Think of a time when you made a conscious decision to change some aspect of your life, *and when you succeeded in making the change.* Why did you want to make the change? What helped you succeed? What difference has it made to your life now? How do you feel about that?

2. Think of a time when you made a conscious decision to change some aspect of your life, *but did not succeed in making the change.* Why did you want to make the change? What got in the way of succeeding? What difference has it made to your life now, that you did not make that change? How do you feel about that?

3. Think of a time when you realised that you had made (or were in the process of making) a significant change in your life, *without having made a conscious or deliberate decision to do so.* Looking back, what were the roots of that change? What or who influenced you? How did it come about? What difference has it made to your life now? How do you feel about that?

4. Thinking of your life now, are there changes you would like to make? What or who could help you? What might get in the way? What difference do you hope these changes will make?

Chapter 4 – How long is 'sustainable'?

Suggestions for reflection (in journalling or creative listening – see appendices – or any other way that works for you)

1. Consider Elise Boulding's suggestion (page 55) that we expand our time horizon by thinking from our grandparents' births to our grandchildren's deaths. What do you know about the time when your grandparents were born? Can you feel it as 'real'? When might be the time of your grandchildren's deaths? If you are too young to be a grandparent, think forward to the time when your potential, as-yet-unborn grandchildren will be old. If you are of 'grandparent age', but don't have grandchildren of your own, think of the grandchildren of someone you know who is about the same age as you. What can you imagine of how the world might be at that time? What might be good or bad about it?

2. Take another look at the climate deadlines on page 63. Thinking of your own life and of the lives of those close to you, what will the dates 02020, 02030, 02050 and 02100 mean to you and to them?

Chapter 5 – We are all crew

Suggestion 1

Take a few moments of quiet to identify a time when you were an apathetic bystander, and another time when you were a bystander who intervened.

Think about the situations; the other people; what you did/didn't do. How did you feel? What happened? What were the outcomes for you? For the others? How do you feel about it now?

If you are doing this with a group, split into threes or fours (not more than four), and take it in turns to share with the others in your group – about 10 minutes each. Explain the story of both events; and as you tell them, try to identify for yourself what made the difference for you between intervening or not.

After this, share in the whole group what made the difference between apathy and intervention.

Referring to page 77, what made the difference for you at step three in the bystander process – the moment of assuming responsibility for the situation? Reflect and discuss.

You might like to relate this to practices of personal discernment, if you are familiar with these.

If you are doing this alone, tell your stories (as above) as you would to a group, but in writing. Then write your reflections on the questions above.

Suggestion 2

Use *lectio divina* or empty-chair Bible study (see appendices) on the Good Samaritan story (see page 70); consider the Earth as being "set upon by thieves".

Chapter 6 – The time is now

1. If you have been using this study guide in a group, use worship-sharing for this session; if you have been using it alone, use reflective writing (see Appendices). Thinking about the series of study sessions as a whole, consider the focusing questions: How am I *feeling* about all this? What am I *thinking* about it? What do I *want to do?*

2. A possible follow-up idea for your meeting might be to conduct a skills audit and then set up some skill-share days. Enquire among older members of the meeting what skills they have, from their youth, that are no longer used. Ask younger members about skills they can teach older people. Ask everyone what practical skills they have – as mundane as darning socks or mending bicycle punctures, or as exotic as . . . you name it! These might be outdoor skills, homemaking, craft, DIY, soft skills (that's people-based skills, such as leadership, facilitation, conflict-handling, etc.), creative skills of all kinds . . . and so on. Once you start, your meeting will discover it has much to share.

APPENDIX I – CREATIVE LISTENING/ WORSHIP-SHARING

Adapted from the online library of Friends General Conference at http://www.fgcquaker.org/ao/worship-sharing. Used with permission.

Worship-sharing is a kind of guided meditation. By focusing on a particular question, it helps us to explore our own experience and share with each other more deeply than we would in normal conversation. It seeks to draw us into sacred space, where we can take down our usual defences and encounter each other in "that which is eternal".

The guidelines for worship-sharing have been evolving among Friends for the past half-century, drawing on a number of different sources. They can be summarised as follows:

1. The convener or leader should define a question as the focus for sharing which is simple, open-ended and oriented toward individual experience. It might be a question about the spiritual journey; it might be related to an issue that is exercising or dividing the meeting; it might arise out of a book you have been reading together. The question should be chosen prayerfully, to meet the particular needs of the group at that time. There are no stock questions.

2. The convener then explains the basic rules for sharing:
   • Reach as deeply as you can into the sacred centre of your life.
   • Speak out of the silence, and leave a period of silence between speakers.
   • Speak from your own experience, about your own experience. Concentrate on feelings and changes rather than on thoughts or theories.
   • Do not respond to what anyone else has said, either to praise or to refute.
   • Listen carefully and deeply to what is spoken. Expect to speak only once, until everyone has had a chance to speak.
   • Respect the confidentiality of what is shared.

3. Some leaders feel that going around the circle makes it easier for everyone to speak. Others prefer to ask people to speak as they are ready. Explain which practice you would like to follow. In either case, participants should know that they have the option of not speaking.

4. Allow at least half an hour for a group of five or six to share their responses to a single question, and at least an hour for a larger group. If you have more than a dozen people, it would be better to divide into smaller groups to make sure that everyone has a chance to participate.

5. Enter into worshipful silence, and begin.

Suggestions for further reading:

Rosalind Priestman, *Listening to one another: Some ideas about creative listening groups and other ways of getting to know one another* (Birmingham: Woodbrooke, 1989).

Daphne Clement, *Group spiritual nurture: The wisdom of spiritual listening* (Wallingford (PA): Pendle Hill, 2004).

APPENDIX 2 – JOURNALLING/PERSONAL REFLECTIVE WRITING

You do not have to be a regular journaller to be able to make creative use of reflective writing. If you are going through a particular life experience, studying something, or taking part in a taught course or group experience, then keeping a notebook – to gather reflections, thoughts, ideas, matters to follow up and so forth – can be helpful. The writing can range from a simple reading diary (what you have read, when you were reading it, anything that struck you about it, quotes you want to remember, things it made you think about), to a gratitudes diary, through to much deeper reflective writing.

If you have never kept a journal, here are some ideas to get you started:

- It is good to have a book to write in, rather than scraps of paper: experience suggests not a loose-leaf file but a notebook; not a shorthand notebook and preferably not anything that reminds you of a school exercise book. Most stationers carry a range of attractive hard-bound notebooks – choose something that appeals to your eye, that will draw you into it. You might want a small book that you carry around with you to use when something comes to mind; or you might prefer a larger one that you can use at home, at a time chosen for quiet writing; or both. Choose what will best suit the realities of your daily life.

- Write direct onto your computer: some people prefer to use a keyboard rather than a pen. Do whatever allows your thoughts and reflections to flow freely.

- If you can't get started, imagine writing an 'unsent letter' to someone: write to someone who will be interested in you and your life and in what you are writing about; a sympathetic listener who will understand and value your thoughts and reflections.

- Don't worry about being grammatical or about spelling properly: you aren't writing for an examination or for a teacher to correct;

write to express yourself and explore; or paint or draw or doodle as well.

- Some people find it helpful as a spiritual discipline to write every day, but don't 'ought' yourself about that; and if you do want to write daily, choose a time that suits your own rhythms. Some people find it helpful to decide a length of time (say, 10 minutes) and then to keep on writing for that time, no matter what comes out on the page; experiment with what works for you.

- Christina Baldwin says: "Here are the rules about journalling – always put the date on everything you write; there are no other rules."

- Enjoy it!

Other resources on journalling

Christina Baldwin, *Life's companion: Journal writing as a spiritual practice*, revised edition (New York: Bantam Books, 2007).

Julia Cameron, *The artist's way: A spiritual path to higher creativity* (London: Pan, 1995). See especially the section on 'morning pages', or go to http://paperartstudio.tripod.com/artistsway/id3.html.

APPENDIX 3 – LECTIO DIVINA

Adapted with permission from: Chris Cook and Brenda Heales, Seeding the Spirit: The Appleseed workbook *(Birmingham: Woodbrooke, 2001).*

Introduction

Lectio divina or 'holy reading' is a way of praying which has come to us from the early Benedictine monasteries in the fifth century. It remains a central part of the daily prayer life of such monasteries to this day. Daily reading has always been part of the devotional practice of monks and nuns; it was a practice that could very easily become routine. *Lectio divina* was devised as a way of keeping the reading living and relevant. Its structured approach to a short piece of text made it possible for the words to take on new life, as the reader was able get in touch with the Spirit which gave them forth.

The traditional *lectio* passes through four stages:

Lectio – reading, to receive the meaning of the passage and clarify difficulties;

Meditatio – reflection on the passage, chewing it over, saying the words aloud and 'tasting' them;

Oratio – allowing the heart to be touched, noticing where emotions are stirred;

Contemplatio – letting one word or short phrase arise, and repeating this over until silence and emptiness take hold.

The form of *lectio* below is one that Appleseed has evolved, although its roots are in the traditional practice.

You will need at least half an hour for the exercise. You could take up to an hour, partly depending on the length of the passage you have chosen. Be flexible to your own needs.

Before sitting down to the *lectio*, you will need to have chosen a passage which you are going to use as your focus. You could choose something from the Bible or from *Quaker faith and practice*. It could be an excerpt from a book you have found helpful or challenging; it could be a short poem, or a verse or verses from a longer poem. If you choose prose, keep the piece down to one or two paragraphs, a maximum of, say, 25 lines.

Immediately before doing the *lectio* allow time to centre down, to be quiet and still.

Stage 1

Read the passage through for its general meaning and begin to explore what it is about. If there are any difficult words or concepts, spend a moment trying to understand them. If you still cannot decipher the meanings decide not to worry, but to check them out after the exercise.

Stage 2

Say the words aloud enjoying and focusing on their sounds, their rhythm and any rhyme they may have. (If you are doing this in a group, you will need to repeat your words in a stage whisper rather than declaim them – with everyone in the room doing this together, you'll find you won't feel self-conscious).

Stage 3

Visualise the scene the words create. This can be one scene depicted by the whole passage, or it could be a part. Even some short phrases, or one word, may give you a strong visual image.

Stage 4

Re-read the passage slowly, letting your mind be attracted to single words or phrases that perhaps interest, excite, repel, challenge or disturb you. Think of it as letting these words 'choose you' because they have energy for you; they nudge you even if you don't know why.

Stage 5

Hold one or two words in concentration. Exclude everything else. Repeat them over and over.

Stage 6
Wait until silence and emptiness fill your mind.

At the end of the exercise you may wish to:

- remain in silence for a time
- write something (some random jottings, or something more struc-tured)
- draw something or make an image (see below*).

Whatever you choose to do, close the exercise by reading the passage through once more.

If working together in a group with others, take a period of shar-ing, followed by silence to close.

---

* **You might want to ensure that you have available:**
- Drawing and writing paper
- A pen, and maybe additional coloured pens
- Pencils: plain lead and coloured
- Pastels (these are particularly useful for covering paper quickly)
- Felt pens

APPENDIX 4 – EMPTY-CHAIR BIBLE STUDY
(*with thanks to Lizz Roe*)

As with *lectio divina*, this can be used with non-biblical material.

Stage one
Choose a passage you are going to use – don't make it too long, not more than a couple of paragraphs.

Stage 2
Seat the group in a horseshoe and have one extra empty chair.

Stage 3
Read the passage around the group a couple of times, leaving time for bits to sink in and to reflect on – this is especially important if it's a longer passage.

Stage 4
Anyone can now ask a question of the text. This means that anyone in the group can ask a question of any of the characters, or even inanimate objects, in the text. For example, in the Good Samaritan text someone might ask what it was like to be the priest passing by, what he felt, what he was thinking about, where he was going, etc.

Stage 5
After someone has asked a question, anyone can answer it by going and sitting in the empty chair. More than one person can answer the same question, one after the other.

Asking and answering questions can go on for a while, perhaps for a length of time that you've agreed in advance.

Stage 6
It's useful to have a short period of worship-sharing about the experience at the end.

One of the many good things about this format for Bible study is that it works for both those very familiar with the text and those who are new to it. It works if there are people with scholarly understanding, and for those with a devotional approach to scripture. And it can mean that texts that seem very familiar suddenly open up in new ways.

PERMISSIONS